EXPERIENCING GOD
in the ORDINARY

Other Loyola Press Books by
William A. Barry

Letting God Come Close: An Approach to the Ignatian Spiritual Exercises

A Friendship Like No Other: Experiencing God's Amazing Embrace

God's Passionate Desire

Here's My Heart, Here's My Hand: Living Fully in Friendship with God

Changed Heart, Changed World: The Transforming Freedom of Friendship with God

Praying the Truth: Deepening Your Friendship with God through Honest Prayer

An Invitation to Love: A Personal Retreat on the Great Commandment

EXPERIENCING GOD
in the ORDINARY

WILLIAM A. BARRY, SJ

LOYOLA PRESS.
A JESUIT MINISTRY
Chicago

LOYOLA PRESS.
A JESUIT MINISTRY

3441 N. Ashland Avenue
Chicago, Illinois 60657
(800) 621-1008
www.loyolapress.com

Imprimi potest: Very Rev. John J. Cecero, SJ

Cover art credit: Oleh_Slobodeniuk/E+/Getty Images.

ISBN: 978-0-8294-5033-0
Library of Congress Control Number: 2019955328

Printed in the United States of America.
20 21 22 23 24 25 26 27 28 29 Versa 10 9 8 7 6 5 4 3 2 1

To Mary and John Power,
Signs of God's Presence in So Many Ways

Teach me to seek you,
and reveal yourself to me as I seek;
for unless you instruct me
I cannot seek you,
and unless you reveal yourself
I cannot find you.

Let me seek you in desiring you;
let me desire you in seeking you.
Let me find you in loving you;
let me love you in finding you.

—St. Anselm of Canterbury

Contents

Preface

On a recent retreat a man said, "I had come to believe that I had achieved all the insights into God I would ever have and had become rather content to rest on these insights only to have Jesus tell me, 'We're not finished yet.'" He realized that he had been presumptuous. Jesus was reminding him that God is ever greater than any insights we might have. As he told his story, I felt a bell ring for me; through him God seemed to be telling me that we are not finished either. Since you have picked up this book, it may be that God is telling you that he is not finished with you. This little story gives you some idea of what I will be talking about throughout the book. It is an instance of my experiencing God through the words or actions of another human being.

Often, we think that we must go to some specific place to find God. Even that last phrase, "to find God," may get us off on the wrong foot. These words can give the impression that God is lost and we've got to find him. But this universe is God's dwelling place because the act of creation is ongoing. If God were to stop creating the universe, there would be nothing except God. Indeed, it may be that God would not be God if he were to regret creating our world and give up creating. God is, in some mysterious way, present everywhere in creation. We don't have to find a special place where he is.

Truth be told, there are places that may make it easier for us to recognize the presence of God. Something about a particular place—say, the Grand Canyon or a mountain range or a lovely seascape—grabs our attention in such a way that we forget our cares and concerns, and God can penetrate our consciousness. Such natural or human-made scenes are called "thin places" by the Irish. It seems that in such places the membrane that separates us from God's presence is thin enough that God can break into our consciousness more easily.

That being said, I want to underline that everywhere can be, and often is, a "thin place" for us. *Our God is a lover of the ordinary*, you might say. As you read and pray, I hope you will come to agree, having discovered for yourself how often you have been surprised by God in your ordinary, daily life.

I urge you to take seriously your own experience as you go through this book with me. I will be sharing experiences I have had, experiences others have shared with me, and stories I have picked up in newspapers, novels, poems, and books. I hope that these various experiences will remind you of events and experiences in your own life that you can see, at least in retrospect, were instances of meeting God in the ordinary events of life.

If you join me, we will embark together on a journey of learning more about the Mystery we call God. I hope that you will take my invitation very seriously, expecting to be surprised by what we discover together and following your own leads to experiences and movements of heart and mind that go beyond any I point you to. I approach this project with a hope that I will, in the course of writing, be surprised by God and discover new insights. Perhaps you can engage in this reading with the same hope. Thus, together we will come to know more about God and ourselves through paying attention to our experience.

Throughout I will encourage you to talk with and listen to God. If this kind of conversational prayer is strange to you, you might be helped by reading either of two books on prayer I've written: *God and You: Prayer as a Personal Relationship* (New York/Mahwah, NJ: Paulist Press, 1987); or *Praying the Truth: Deepening Your Friendship with God through Honest Prayer* (Chicago: Loyola Press, 2012).

1

How Ordinary Was Jesus?

During the past Easter season (2019), I was struck by how ordinary the various appearances of the risen Jesus actually were. There is nothing at all written about Jesus' resurrection itself. We are told only about his empty tomb. When Jesus does appear, he is unrecognizable at first, even to his closest friends.

Moreover, the appearances are rather ordinary: he walks along with two disciples on the road to Emmaus; Mary Magdalene thinks he must be a gardener; he enters the upper room and asks for something to eat; he stands on the seashore and tells the disciples who have caught no fish to try the other side of the boat; on the shore he has some fish already cooked and tells Peter to get some more from that catch. In most cases, his friends finally recognize him by some familiar word or gesture: he says Mary's name; he breaks bread and hands it to the two disciples who met him on the road to Emmaus; he helps the disciples catch fish; he shows his friends the wounds in his hands and side.

Admittedly, it's way out of the ordinary to meet, alive and well, someone you saw die in a horrible way. Still, in these accounts of the risen Jesus, there are no big displays of power or majesty or glory; there is nothing newsworthy, you might say, in these stories. A publicist would have nightmares with the ordinariness of it all, wondering how he is to get the story across to the larger public.

Once I began thinking about the everyday-ness of the Resurrection stories, I realized that the whole of Jesus' life is rather ordinary. God became a human being, and all we know of the first thirty or so years of his life is a few stories from his birth and another from the time he was about twelve. Even the three years of his public life are not especially spectacular. Israel was not the center of things in any sense most people of that day would accept. Like many other small and large countries, it was controlled by the Roman Empire. In this small and out-of-the-way land, Jesus gathered a few disciples around him and tried, without much success, to get them to understand who God is and what it meant for Jesus himself to be the promised Messiah. He cured a number of people—which, in that time and place, was not out of the ordinary for a "holy person." Like many a prophet and preacher before and since, he announced the imminent coming of the kingdom of God and got into trouble with the leaders of his own religion. After three or fewer years of public life, Jesus of Nazareth was handed over by those leaders to the Roman governor to be crucified as a common criminal. To most observers of the time, Jesus was simply another failed, would-be leader. A publicist would have little reason to make Jesus' story known. Even after the Resurrection, Jesus appeared only to his followers—he made no dramatic or miraculous appearances that might wow and convert people in the general public.

I believe that the ordinariness of Jesus' life, death, and post-resurrection appearances tells us something profound about God. God does not need to be flashy to prove anything to us. Nor does Jesus, God's Son. God just *is* and acts, and he leaves it to us to recognize who he is and what he has done. God is not in competition with us or with any other part of creation. God loves the world as it is, in all its ordinariness. Perhaps this love of the ordinary explains God's predilection in the Old Testament for the weak and lost, the widow, the orphan, and the poor. Moreover, it is enough for God to become a human being in Jesus of Nazareth to transform the world, without having to make a big splash. God is God, and that's enough.

What this means, however, is that everything changes for us who live in this world where God is present now as one of us. The whole universe is different because now God is in some mysterious but very real way part of the universe itself, with a body that is related to everything else in the universe. This means that everything is touched by God's bodily presence in the universe. So, when the poet and farmer Wendell Berry imagines going out to his barn and there encountering the holy family, he is speaking a truth. And when the poet Gerard Manley Hopkins writes, "The world is charged with the grandeur of God," he, too, is making a truth claim *about the real world we all inhabit.* The ordinary things of this world are transformed by Jesus' presence in it.

I press this point because I want to help readers notice the surprising ways in which we encounter this mysterious presence of God. I am convinced that all of us meet God regularly and in quite ordinary ways. The question is, do we notice this when it happens?

A Great Endeavor, Indeed

I use the words *great endeavor* advisedly. We are, after all, invited by God to join in the great endeavor that is this real world of which we are a part. For too long, religion has been associated with retreat from the world—indeed, with contempt for the world. God has no such contempt for the world God creates. In the first chapter of Genesis, the first story of creation, six times we read that God "saw that it was good," and after the creation of human beings we read that God "saw everything that he had made, and indeed, it was very good." In the book of Wisdom we read:

> For you love all things that exist,
> and detest none of the things that you have made,
> for you would not have made anything if you had
>   hated it.
> How would anything have endured if you had not
>   willed it?
> Or how would anything not called forth by you have
>   been preserved?
> You spare all things, for they are yours, O Lord, you
>   who love the living.

> —Wisdom 11:24–26

The most famous line in John's Gospel (and perhaps in the whole Bible) is John 3:16: "For God so loved the world that he gave his only Son, so that everyone who believes in him may not perish but may have eternal life." Indeed we can say, and rightly, God loved this ordinary, messy, imperfect world so much that he gave his only Son to become one with it, to take part in its messiness and imperfection—and to become so involved in its broken life that he ended up dying a death of low status and high shame, although he'd done nothing to deserve such treatment. That's how much God loves this world!

Let me give you an example of God showing up in an ordinary event. Carl Scovel, former pastor of King's Chapel in Boston, gave a five-minute sermon every Sunday from 1979 to 1999 on WCRB, a classical music station in the Boston area. The best of these talks have been collected in his book *Never Far from Home: Stories from the Radio Pulpit*.[1] In it, he tells the story of a Christmas midnight service at his sister's parish in England. The service was conducted without any music or singing, but as the people received communion, they heard a drunken voice singing "You'll Never Walk Alone" from Rodgers and Hammerstein's *Carousel*. The voice seemed to come from within the church, but they could see no one. It turned out that the vicar's lapel microphone had picked up the sound from a pub next door. The vicar said, "Well, we could do a lot worse. . . . The man's right, you know. We don't ever walk anywhere alone, because Jesus is always walking with us."[2]

You may be thinking that it was mere coincidence that the drunken man sang that song and the vicar's microphone picked it up. It may have been a coincidence, but who is to say that that coincidence cannot also be a sign of God's presence for the vicar and for those who were open to believing in the presence of God everywhere? Just as a rose means different things to different people but to a believer is also a sign of the creative beauty of God, for us who believe, events that have many explanations, including coincidence, can be signs of God-with-us. Of course, we need to be discerning about events and what in them is indicative of God's presence, but nonetheless, for those who believe in God, God is present everywhere and in every event. In this book's final chapter, I will offer some thoughts on how to discern what indicates the presence of God.

The Sign of Hearts on Fire

You remember the Emmaus story in Luke's Gospel, I'm sure. But to refresh your memory here it is. It's the third day after Jesus' cruel death on a cross. Two of Jesus' disciples have left Jerusalem bound for Emmaus, very disheartened despite some stories they have heard of the empty tomb.

Now on that same day two of them were going to a village called Emmaus, about seven miles from Jerusalem,

and talking with each other about all these things that
had happened. While they were talking and discussing,
Jesus himself came near and went with them, but their
eyes were kept from recognizing him. And he said to
them, "What are you discussing with each other while
you walk along?" They stood still, looking sad. Then one
of them, whose name was Cleopas, answered him, "Are
you the only stranger in Jerusalem who does not know
the things that have taken place there in these days?" He
asked them, "What things?" They replied, "The things
about Jesus of Nazareth, who was a prophet mighty in
deed and word before God and all the people, and how
our chief priests and leaders handed him over to be condemned to death and crucified him. But we had hoped
that he was the one to redeem Israel. Yes, and besides
all this, it is now the third day since these things took
place. Moreover, some women of our group astounded
us. They were at the tomb early this morning, and when
they did not find his body there, they came back and
told us that they had indeed seen a vision of angels who
said that he was alive. Some of those who were with us
went to the tomb and found it just as the women had
said; but they did not see him." Then he said to them,
"Oh, how foolish you are, and how slow of heart to
believe all that the prophets have declared! Was it not
necessary that the Messiah should suffer these things and
then enter into his glory?" Then beginning with Moses

and all the prophets, he interpreted to them the things about himself in all the scriptures.

As they came near the village to which they were going, he walked ahead as if he were going on. But they urged him strongly, saying, "Stay with us, because it is almost evening and the day is now nearly over." So he went in to stay with them. When he was at the table with them, he took bread, blessed and broke it, and gave it to them. Then their eyes were opened, and they recognized him; and he vanished from their sight. They said to each other, "Were not our hearts burning within us while he was talking to us on the road, while he was opening the scriptures to us?" That same hour they got up and returned to Jerusalem; and they found the eleven and their companions gathered. They were saying, "The Lord has risen indeed, and he has appeared to Simon!" Then they told what had happened on the road, and how he had been made known to them in the breaking of the bread. (Luke 24:13–35)

What I want to underline in this story is the fact that their hearts were burning as the stranger explained the Scriptures to them; however, they did not pay attention to those burning hearts until after Jesus broke the bread, a familiar gesture that opened their eyes. I hope your eyes are more open than theirs were, so that you will notice more readily that your heart is often burning and that you are in the presence of God. You may be surprised at how frequently in a day you meet God, and often in the oddest of circumstances.

A Different Way to Look Back on Your Day

In my own life I have become more open to noticing God's presence by engaging once again in an ancient practice, the examination of consciousness. When I entered the Jesuits in 1950, we were all introduced to the practice of this examination. Bells rang twice a day, at noon and just before bedtime, to remind us to engage in it. However, I have to admit that relatively soon after the bells stopped ringing, I seemed to have dropped the practice. I had bouts of guilt feelings that got me trying it again, but in time it had passed from my regular practice. As I look back now, I believe that I stopped the practice because it was disheartening and tedious and led to too much self-absorption. Moreover, it became, like my regular confessions, repetitious and self-focused as I continually found myself absorbed in petty faults.

In recent years I have returned to the *examen*, and it has been invigorating and transforming. I have spent the time asking God to let me see what I am grateful for since I last said this prayer. I don't spend time on my sins. They come to mind quite easily when I look over the day, with God's help, to see what I am grateful for.

Over the years since I have taken up this kind of *examen* of consciousness, I have become more attuned to noticing the presence of God at the time when "my heart is burning"—that is, in the actual moment. In addition, it has given me fodder for good conversations with God. In other words, without my intending it, I have become more aware of God during the day. I hope I am moving in the direction of becoming a "contemplative in action," an ideal in Ignatian spirituality. And it has happened without any heavy lifting on my part. Try it. You may like it.

Many of the examples used in this book have come to me through my daily *examen*s. If you try this kind of *examen* and find it helpful to you, there will be an extra dividend to my practice. Again, you will notice that many of the stories provide extra dividends, dividends probably not in the mind of those who originally told the stories or did the actions described. As we become alert to the God of surprises, we will see how God's actions have such multiplier effects. So, stay alert! You'll be surprised at what you notice.

2

Mustard Seeds, Yeast, and Other Tiny Things

In Luke's Gospel, Jesus tells his disciples about the kingdom of God through two images:

> He said therefore, "What is the kingdom of God like? And to what should I compare it? It is like a mustard seed that someone took and sowed in the garden; it grew and became a tree, and the birds of the air made nests in its branches."
>
> And again he said, "To what should I compare the kingdom of God? It is like yeast that a woman took and mixed in with three measures of flour until all of it was leavened." (Luke 13:18–21)

First of all notice that Jesus is speaking of the kingdom *of God*. Jesus, and other Jewish people who took the Scriptures seriously, believed that God had a purpose in creation.

Jesus called this purpose "the kingdom of God." I have come to believe that what he meant by the term is that God wants a world in which human beings live in harmony with God and with one another and with the whole of creation. Notice that I have stressed "of God." When times are tough, we can easily forget that the one who wants the kingdom to come is God—and what God wants, God achieves. If we come to such faith in God, then we will never be overcome by despair or hopelessness, no matter how bad things look.

Such faith in God has great relevance for us who live in what seems to be a very dangerous time indeed, a time when optimism is no easy option. Such times test our faith in God. When I was provincial superior of the Jesuits of New England, I said something like the following to our province assembly that fits here. I said it with some humor but also quite seriously.

> When most of us entered the Society of Jesus, we didn't have to believe in God; we could believe in the Church which was growing by leaps and bounds; or we could believe in the Society of Jesus which, in the United States, was growing very fast. Now [around 1995] we have a chance to find out whether we believe in God.

What I meant was that, since the early 1970s, the growth of both the church and the Society had slowed remarkably.

The average age of the diocesan clergy and of the Jesuits in the United States had climbed very perceptibly. Things have not changed for the better for the church and the Jesuits in the United States since then.

The question all of us must face is, Do I believe in God? To believe in God means that we believe that God's dream for our world is still alive and well, no matter how dark it seems, because God is God. Remember that when Julian of Norwich was near death, and all around her people were dying of the Black Plague, she heard the words, "All shall be well, and all shall be well, and all manner of thing shall be well."

The second thing to notice in Jesus' statement in Luke 13 is that, in both examples he gives, something tiny does great things. The tiny mustard seed becomes a tree that provides housing for many birds. The bit of yeast slowly leavens the whole loaf. Despite any evidence to the contrary, small things and small gestures matter a great deal. In the chapters to come, I will concentrate on small events—small events that showed the face of God to others and thus had a positive effect on some part of the world. Inspired by the Spirit of God, these "tiny things" join with all the other small events inspired by the Spirit to form the great stream that is God's one action in creation.

A third thing to note is that the mustard seed and the yeast, though near invisible, are acting all the time to produce their results, at least when they are in their proper environments. These homely illustrations remind us that God is always present and working in this world to bring about what God intends in creation.

In the last prayer session suggested by Ignatius of Loyola to those who make his *Spiritual Exercises*, the retreatants ask to experience God as dwelling in all creatures and as working on our behalf in all creatures (*Sp. Ex.* 235, 236). The two images Jesus uses to describe the kingdom of God thus call attention to the fact that God is always dwelling with us and working with us to bring about God's dream for our world. For a believer the world is, in the words of Gerard Manley Hopkins, "charged with the grandeur of God." In a real sense, we are always in the presence of God because there is no place in this world from which God is absent. Moreover, God is always working to draw us toward cooperating with the divine purpose and intention in creation.

I want to help you notice God's presence and activity in your daily life. In addition, I hope to encourage you to be what you are created to be, an image of God in this world and thus a presence of God to others in God's great adventure, which is ongoing creation.

By the way, that poem of Hopkins goes on to describe how smeared and bleared the world is by all that we humans have done. Yet this poet, so prone to melancholy and depression, could finish his poem with these lines:

> And for all this, nature is never spent;
>> There lives the dearest freshness deep down things;
> And though the last lights off the black West went
>> Oh, morning, at the brown brink eastward,
>>> springs—
> Because the Holy Ghost over the bent
>> World broods with warm breast and with ah!
>>> bright wings.

Hopkins's faith in God enabled him to sense the presence of God in all things. His poetry helps us see the deep darkness that plagued him all his life, but it also reveals, in stunning detail, how often he was surprised by God through the ordinary things and ordinary people he encountered.

The Contagion of Goodness

Jesus' images of a mustard seed and yeast can also point to another aspect of how the kingdom of God develops. I am convinced that the presence of God is something like an infectious disease that is passed from person to person, only here it is a contagion of goodness. Notice how many people were affected by Jesus himself and then by his early followers.

Indeed, in *The Rise of Christianity*, sociologist Rodney Stark contends that the extraordinarily quick rise of Christianity in the early centuries of our era can be attributed to such a contagion. Among other factors he singles out the fact that in the plagues that regularly and often afflicted the large cities of the Roman Empire, Christians and their neighbors in larger numbers survived the plagues better than did non-Christians. The Christians took more care of one another and even of their non-Christian neighbors. It is now a known reality that care, even if there is no medical intervention, does have a healing effect on those who are cared for. The non-Christians noted this difference in survival and were thus attracted to Christianity.

A famous example of the contagion of goodness is the effect Monica had on her son Augustine. In my own religious congregation, the Society of Jesus, a notable example of the contagion of holiness occurred when Ignatius of Loyola became a roommate of Pierre Favre and Francis Xavier. Ignatius's example drew, first Pierre, and more slowly, Francis, to make the *Spiritual Exercises* and afterward to join with Ignatius and others to form the Society of Jesus. All three are now saints in the church. What we will notice often in these pages is how surprise meetings with God through other people have a ripple effect.

The idea for this contagion concept came to me during a very moving luncheon while I was writing this book. Darrell Jones was imprisoned for thirty-two years for a murder he did not commit. His original conviction was voided in December 2017, the judge ruling that there was racial bias in the jury and that the principal detective in the case had lied under oath.

At the time of this lunch, Darrell had been out of prison for eleven months and was living in my Jesuit community while awaiting the final disposition of his case. (In June of 2019, at his retrial, the jury returned a "not guilty" verdict.) He and I had lunch with Mary Richardson, her husband, Stan Leven, and Kathy Bickimer. These three, all of whom were connected at one time with WCVB TV of Boston's ongoing program *Chronicle*, had played a significant role in the unfolding of Darrell's case. As we neared the end of our lunch, Darrell spoke very movingly about why he wanted to meet the other three, and he spoke of the contagion of love.

I became involved with Darrell through Fr. George Zahl, a former student of mine at Weston Jesuit School of Theology, who was a chaplain at Darrell's prison. Darrell is not a Catholic, but he got involved with Fr. Zahl when, on his way to the gym, he heard that Mother Teresa of Calcutta was visiting the prison. On a whim he decided to join the group she was with. Thus, as he says, he got to meet a saint and was blessed by her, and he also got involved in helping Fr. Zahl with the music for his services.

When Darrell was feeling very down and in solitary confinement, he asked Fr. Zahl if he knew someone who was a believer and a psychologist to whom he could write. Fr. Zahl thought of me, called me, and told me what Darrell wanted. Because I fit the bill, I agreed. Darrell wrote to me, and I responded. Eventually I started to visit him, and other things began to happen. I found out that the Innocence Program of Massachusetts was now expanding its scope to take on cases in which DNA was not a factor. That program took on Darrell's case and started a process that eventually led to his release.

I also had my regular life going on and had become a friend of Mary Richardson. At a previous lunch with her, I mentioned Darrell and his case and also that he was working with other prisoners to try to make things better in the neighborhoods from which they came. Mary told her husband, Stan Leven, a producer at *Chronicle*, and the two of them showed interest in what Darrell was doing from prison. This led to their filming Mary interviewing Darrell and other prisoners inside the prison and the production of a *Chronicle* story featuring these prisoners' work for others. Mary and Stan continued their interest in Darrell's case, and that interest was taken up by another producer at *Chronicle*, Kathy Bickimer, who produced three shows on Darrell's trial and final release.

Now you know why all of us at the lunch eleven months after his release were so moved and why Darrell spoke of the contagion of love. I hope you noticed how one good event or deed led to another with remarkable results. I am convinced that the contagion of love will continue to affect others. Darrell as a free man will have a great positive effect on many other people. Indeed, he is already having such an effect.

Tolkien and the Hobbits

At this point I cannot resist mentioning a literary instance of the kind of contagion I mean. It runs almost as a theme through J.R.R. Tolkien's remarkable imaginative achievement *The Hobbit* and its three companion novels collectively titled *The Lord of the Rings*. In *The Hobbit*, Bilbo Baggins is the title character. Hobbits are small folk who live simple lives among elves, dwarves, wizards, and Big People (humans) in Tolkien's Middle-earth. Bilbo has a cousin named Frodo, who becomes the central character in the trilogy, *The Lord of the Rings*. Many of you know this story through the movies made of the novels some years ago. For my purposes here, I need to summarize in brief detail.

In the time before Bilbo, the evil Dark Lord Sauron had forged a number of rings of power, one of them being the ring of greatest power. In one of the many wars caused by Sauron's thirst for all power, this ring was lost, seemingly forever. However, it had been found by a strange character named Sméagol, or Gollum, and became his "Precious," enjoyed in his underground lair. As happens to anyone who wears this ring for any time, Gollum became addicted to it. In *The Hobbit*, Bilbo, by accident, finds the ring and keeps it against the will of Gollum. At one point, moved by compassion, Bilbo turns away from killing Gollum. When Bilbo returns to his home in the Shire, he enjoys great prosperity and renown for his stories.

The Lord of the Rings takes up the story of the ring. Sauron has found out about Bilbo and the ring and is seeking him out. Bilbo, at the urging of the wizard Gandalf, makes Frodo his heir and at his "eleventy-first birthday party" disappears mysteriously, leaving Frodo with the ring. Thus begins the long story of the growth of opposing armies, those of Sauron and those who oppose him.

The main thread, however, is the quest of Frodo and his faithful servant Sam to bring the ring to the fires of Mount Doom, into which they must throw the ring, thus destroying it forever and saving the world from the domination of Sauron. Gollum, however, is still addicted to the ring and follows Frodo and Sam along their perilous journey. At one point, Frodo and Sam capture Gollum. Just as Bilbo, in *The Hobbit*, had decided not to kill Gollum when provoked, so, too, in the trilogy, Frodo, out of compassion, spares Gollum's life. Moreover, at one point, the elves, who are on the side of the good, spare Gollum because they do not know for sure whose side he is on.

Thus, at least three times in the novels, Gollum's life is spared because people act out of compassion—they act as people made in God's image. Rather amazingly, those acts of kindness and compassion are the key to the saving of the world.

At the end, Frodo finds himself addicted to the ring's temptation to power and cannot bring himself to throw it into the fires of Mount Doom. At that very moment, Gollum sneaks up on Frodo, bites off his ring finger, and in a frenzy of joy at having his "Precious" back, loses his balance and falls into the fires of Mount Doom, thus saving the world. Tolkien never mentions God in the set of novels, but clearly the thought of God's providence was one of the deepest founts of his creative work. The message, you might say, is that love and goodwill triumph, but in surprising ways.

Instances of the contagion of goodness, by the way, seem to have been given to us humans and, indeed, to all creatures with our biological natures. In *Mama's Last Hug: Animal Emotions and What They Tell Us about Ourselves*, Frans de Waal demonstrates that what looks like empathy and compassion can be found in monkeys, apes, and even elephants. He speaks of the contagion of such positive emotions in animals as well as in humans. He notes that these findings run counter to the prevailing scientific opinion that the animal and human worlds are governed by a dog-eat-dog mentality. I take it that God has endowed us with biological equipment that moves us toward cooperation with and empathy toward others, something necessary for the survival of all animal species.

I hope you will notice how often in the stories of this book small things and events and actions have surprising effects and signal the presence of God. Despite how awful things seem at times, a bit of kindness and care take on more and more momentum over time and do contribute to the ongoing work of God which is our world and the whole of creation. God is both surprising and enterprising in the ways he infects our world with his love.

3

God Meets Us in Human Love

Fr. Michael Himes, a theology professor at Boston College, said in class, "The least wrong way to imagine God, the Christian tradition says, is to think of God as love." He was, I presume, making two points at least: God is love, yes, but remember that anything we say positively about God can never be the whole story, because God is Mystery itself. The first point merely echoes the words of the First Letter of John, "God is love, and those who abide in love abide in God, and God abides in them" (1 John 4:16b).

In this chapter we will explore our experiences of human love that brought God's presence to us. To begin, though, let's review some examples in the Scriptures.

The prophet Jeremiah, speaking to the Israelites who had been brought captive to Babylon, wrote, among many other hopeful words, this lovely line, God saying to the Israelites:

"I have loved you with an everlasting love; therefore I have continued my faithfulness to you" (Jeremiah 31:3). Many, many people have heard these words spoken to them directly in their imaginations and were convinced that God did love them. Have you ever had such an experience? If not, perhaps you could ask God to let you hear these words now as spoken to you.

The prophet known as Second Isaiah, speaking also to the exiles in Babylon, said this:

> But now thus says the LORD,
>   he who created you, O Jacob,
>   he who formed you, O Israel:
> Do not fear, for I have redeemed you;
>   I have called you by name, you are mine.
> When you pass through the waters, I will be
>   with you;
>   and through the rivers, they shall not
>   overwhelm you;
> when you walk through fire you shall not be burned,
>   and the flame shall not consume you.
> For I am the LORD your God,
>   the Holy One of Israel, your Savior.
> I give Egypt as your ransom,
>   Ethiopia and Seba in exchange for you.
> Because you are precious in my sight,
>   and honored, and I love you,

I give people in return for you,
    nations in exchange for your life.
Do not fear, for I am with you;
    I will bring your offspring from the east,
    and from the west I will gather you;
I will say to the north, "Give them up,"
    and to the south, "Do not withhold;
bring my sons from far away
    and my daughters from the end of the earth—
everyone who is called by my name,
    whom I created for my glory,
    whom I formed and made."

—Isaiah 43:1–7

Imagine this exiled and enslaved people. They knew that their exile and slavery were the result of not listening to the prophets God had sent them prior to and during the approach of the Babylonian armies. Yet now they hear these warm and tender words culminating in the lines "Because you are precious in my sight, and honored, and I love you, I give people in return for you." Can you sense how they felt?

Many, many people have been heartened as they imagined God saying these words to them: "You are precious in my sight, and honored, and I love you." Have you ever had such an experience? If you have, savor that memory, and thank God for speaking so tenderly to you. If not, perhaps you want to ask God now to hear these words spoken to you. Try it and see what happens.

At the Last Supper in John's Gospel, Jesus says to his disciples:

> This is my commandment, that you love one another as I have loved you. No one has greater love than this, to lay down one's life for one's friends. You are my friends if you do what I command you. I do not call you servants any longer, because the servant does not know what the master is doing; but I have called you friends, because I have made known to you everything that I have heard from my Father. (John 15:12–15)

In this passage Jesus tells his disciples, and us, that he loves them and goes on to call them friends. God's love reaches out to us as friendship, a very human concept and experience. For centuries Christians have been heartened by imagining Jesus saying these words directly to them. Again, you may have had such an experience yourself. If so, recall and savor that memory now and thank him for talking to you this way. You have experienced God's presence through the human Jesus. If you have not, perhaps, again, you can ask to hear these words spoken to you in your own imagination. See what happens when you ask.

The Love of Parents for Their Children

So far, we have looked only at direct experience of God's love, but we also have many indirect experiences, don't we? Just think of the love your parents showed you, not only or even mainly, by words, but most especially by deeds. My parents, for example, both immigrants from Ireland, met one another in Worcester, Massachusetts, in the late 1920s. They were married a couple of months after the stock market crash that brought on the Great Depression of 1929 and had me a year later in 1930 at the height of the Depression. My three sisters were born in 1931, 1933, and 1936, all before the Depression broke. What active love it took to bring us into the world and bring us up with my father working at most a couple of days a week at the steel mill near us, and sometimes not at all when his union went on strike!

Like most Americans in those days, we had to scrimp and save in order to make it, but somehow each year my parents took us by train and boat to Nantasket Beach in Hull, Massachusetts, for a week's vacation. My mother, who had been a live-in maid when she first came to the United States, was a great cook and could do marvels with very little, so we never went hungry. My parents made sure that we all went to the parish grammar school and then to Catholic high schools.

They were, for us children, sacraments of God's great love for us, and we have never forgotten that.

In our home God was ever present. We often heard the words *God willing* when a future event was planned, *God bless you* if you sneezed, and other such sayings. We prayed the family rosary every day and most days went to daily Mass. I remember going with my mother to daily Mass in a nearby Lithuanian church in high school and college. In a real way my parents lived close to God and, as a result, so did we children.

Perhaps this personal story reminds you of your own parents' active love for you and how God showed you his love through them. If, like me, your parents are deceased, you can thank them in prayer, assuming that they are now with God. If your parents are still alive, ask yourself when was the last time you thanked them for all the love they showed you. I know I regret not telling my parents often enough how grateful I was to them. But I sense now that they are just happy that I have grown up to be of some help to others as they were great helps to me.

Perhaps you did not experience enough love from your parents. I hope that in the course of your life, you have found people who loved you for who you were and thus were images of God for you.

One's First Love as a Teenager

Can you remember your first love outside the family and how you felt when that love was reciprocated? Wasn't it stunning to find that someone you were attracted to was also attracted to you and liked you? Did you ever think that God was a part of it? I know I didn't, but now I tend to think that such love is a sign of God's love for us.

After all, even if that love was immature and did not last forever, as many first loves do not, still her love for me gave me confidence in myself, and I believe that God wants us to feel confident in ourselves as loveable human beings. After all, that's what we are in God's eyes. And, as difficult as this is for me to believe, perhaps my love for that girl gave her confidence and was a sign of God's love for her, whether she thought of God or not.

Isn't that something to savor, that your teenage love for someone else, as immature as it most likely was, was also a signal of God's so much greater love for the person? Maybe you want to talk to God about these thoughts and memories.

———

In *A Book of Uncommon Prayer: 100 Celebrations of the Miracle & Muddle of the Ordinary,* Brian Doyle has a lovely prayer that may move you to pray for those first loves. Here is part of it:

Prayer of Thanks for Old Girlfriends, or Boyfriends, as the Case May Be

No, we don't think about them much if at all anymore, and yes, it all worked out right that we are not together, and no, it would not have been a good idea at all to continue on in what became a murky emotional wilderness, but yes, we should be grateful that they came into our lives, or that we blundered into theirs; for in many ways they are how we came to be who we are, isn't that so? And didn't we learn how to love better by loving generally poorly and awkwardly in the opening chapters, before moving up to the current big leagues? . . . So thank You for the pain and confusion and thrill of first and second and third loves; thank You for letting us muddle along learning to be painfully honest and not try to be cool and not hold on desperately to that which is rightfully leaving the scene; thank You for the bruise of education, and the joy of the much deeper confusion of marriage. Deft work there, Friend. And so, amen.[3]

Friends as Images of God's Love

Now I would have us think of our closest friends over the years. Take some time to remember them, picture them, and realize what they have meant to you and you to them.

I have been blessed with strong friends all my life. Three of my best friends from high school remained friends until they died, even though we did not see one another often over the years. Whenever we met, we clicked and could easily pick up where we left off. I have a treasured picture of the four of us at the fiftieth reunion of our class. The four of us really gave one another a boost of self-confidence during those high school years through our open friendship and clear liking for one another. I would say that we were a sign of God's love for one another, wouldn't you?

What friendships stand out for you? You might have long-lasting friendships that began when you were quite young. Other important friendships might have developed more recently. As you reflect on your friendships, what signs of God's love can you identify?

After my first three years in the Society of Jesus, I was sent to study philosophy in a small town outside Munich, Germany, from 1953 to 1956. During those years, my best friend was a German Jesuit, Adolph Heuken. I don't know how the two of us hit it off, but we did.

Once a year we took a tandem bike for a day trip to various parts of the Bavarian Alps, covering over a hundred miles on each day trip. Adolph always rode in front and steered and, of course, dictated how long we would keep pumping uphill when we got near the mountains. So I trusted him implicitly on what could be rather dangerous climbs and even more dangerous downhills. I would always be the first to call it quits on the uphill jaunts, and Adolph, with some reluctance, gave in to my pleading to stop. Through him I also got to be friends with his close friends from his home province. One result of these friendships was a pretty good grasp of conversational German. I still remember those years with fondness and am grateful to Adolph for reaching out to me. He was a sign of God's great love for me; I hope I was such a sign for him and my other brother Jesuits at Berchmanskolleg.

When we finished our studies, Adolph was sent to Indonesia, where he remained until his death on July 25, 2019, as I was putting the finishing touches on this book. (May he rest in peace!) I came back to the States. Some ten years later, after both of us were ordained priests, Adolph was given a chance to come to the United States for a few months. I was studying clinical psychology at the University of Michigan. He stopped in Ann Arbor for a couple of days, and we picked up as though we had been in regular contact, which we had not. It was a moving experience for me to realize that friendships can last even without frequent contact. With the advent of e-mail, we were in contact, but not often. He remains for me a sign of God's love.

My high school friends and Adolph, and many other friends, know my strengths and my weaknesses, as I know theirs. Yet we have continued to love one another. That's the way it is with God, who knows even more of our flaws and sins than our closest friends.

Have these stories brought back memories for you? Can you, too, see how friends have been a sign of God's love for you? Can you also trust that you have been a sign of God's love for your friends? Perhaps you have something you want to say to God, who has made such friendships possible.

Being Loved by Someone

Have you ever been overawed by someone's love for you? Can you remember a time when the honest, totally selfless, and undeserved look or expression of love was almost too much to bear? I can remember such looks, and I also remember how I had to deflect the love, usually with some humorous remark. I have also felt the same way when I felt such love from God. I have understood what William Blake meant when he wrote: "We are put on this earth to bear the beams of love." Such beams are often too much to bear. Let me tell you a story from a mother of three boys about whom we will hear again. This one is about her youngest son when he was in kindergarten.

This boy, let's call him Michael, often shows great love for his mother. But this occasion was overwhelming for her. Michael's kindergarten class invited all the mothers to a special treat for Mother's Day. The treat was that the whole kindergarten class sang a song to their mothers. As Michael's mother watched him singing with the other children, she saw such an intense stare of love from Michael that eventually she had to look away for a moment. When she looked back, Michael still had his eyes fixed on her with love. She felt immediately that God was present in her little boy, and both Michael's love and God's were almost too much to bear.

Perhaps this story has reminded you of something similar that has happened to you. If so, you might want to speak to God about the event and your reactions to this memory.

Some years ago, I wrote a series of four articles about the resistance to God's love that can plague us right after we have experienced God's closeness and great love. I mentioned that I once found myself for about two weeks in what I can only call a zone of love, feeling God very close and feeling very much in the moment. But soon this passed. The odd thing is that I never prayed for its return, nor did I even seem to miss that time. I also noticed that whenever someone told me that he or she loved me, I seemed to find myself without words. I might have mumbled thanks but then changed the subject or made some humorous remark. I do find it hard to "bear the beams of love." Perhaps you do too. After a class in which I brought this topic up, I received an anonymous four-page letter listing all the reasons the writer resists the love of God.

Do these stories ring a bell with you? You may want to talk with God about your own reactions, and, if you do find it hard to bear the beams of love, you could ask God's help to be able to bear them more easily. I have found it helpful to admit to God how difficult it is to receive love and to ask God's help to be less afraid. The more open to receiving the love of God and of others, the more kind and caring of others I seem to become. So, let's ask God's help to bear the beams of his love and thus become better images of God, who is love itself.

Spouses as God's Love for One Another

In Isaiah we read:

> You shall no more be termed Forsaken,
>   and your land shall no more be termed Desolate;
> but you shall be called My Delight Is in Her,
>   and your land Married;
> for the LORD delights in you,
>   and your land shall be married.
> For as a young man marries a young woman,

> so shall your builder marry you,
> and as the bridegroom rejoices over the bride,
> so shall your God rejoice over you.
>
> —Isaiah 62:4–5

God speaks to Israel the way a husband might speak to his wife. God *takes delight* in Israel. St. Paul likened the love of Jesus for the people of God to the love between spouses. If you are married, you might reflect on the love you and your spouse have and express for one another as being another example of what God's love looks like and acts like.

The sacrament of marriage is not finished once the marriage ceremony is over. It lasts a lifetime. Spouses vow to love one another through good times and bad until death parts them; such devotion and commitment are signs of God's love for us.

Have you ever spoken to God about your love for your spouse, including your sexual expressions of that love? How did it go? Did you feel as though God was listening and very happy? If you haven't spoken with God, do you want to give it a try now? Go ahead and see what happens.

This prayer for his wife by Brian Doyle may be a help to you in speaking to your own spouse. It's from *A Book of Uncommon Prayer* cited earlier in this chapter.

Prayer for My Lovely Bride
of Twenty-Seven Years

May you always be as vibrant and gracious and tender as you are today. May you never again in this blessed lifetime put milk on to heat for your coffee and turn the burner on high and wander away and get absorbed in something else and have to shriek and sprint into the kitchen as you have every! single! morning! since I met you thirty years ago. May you always be as selflessly engaged and fascinated by other people and unabsorbed by yourself as you are today. May you never again lie awake sleepless worrying that the children's struggles are totally your fault because you were not a good enough mom. May you always have arresting blue-gray eyes exactly the color and potential fury of the sea. May you always be as graciously and kind-heartedly and un-greedily you as you are today. May you someday love yourself as much as I love you. May you, when you finally pass into the next life at age 114, still looking like you are maybe thirty-seven, get total extra credit from the Merciful One for having cheerfully endured marriage to me for so long, though there were endless better candidates for husbandry, handsomer and richer and much more willing to go camping in the muddy sticky insect-ridden wilderness; but, trust me, none of them would have savored and appreciated and celebrated you as much as me. And so: amen.[4]

It may seem strange to think of sexual expression as included in how we reflect and imitate God's love. But God creates human beings with sexual organs and desires. In fact, sexuality permeates all our interactions with the world and especially with other human beings. In some mysterious way, sexuality is familiar to God, not foreign or strange or questionable. We have no idea what this might mean for God; that's part of the mystery of God.

However, in Jesus, God experienced human sexuality and had to learn how to deal with it as he went through his life—as an adolescent but also as a teacher and healer surrounded by crowds and sought after by people with all kinds of motivations. We can talk with Jesus about our own sexuality openly, knowing that he has direct knowledge of what we are talking about. The issue, for us, is how to let God help us grow into mature sexual human beings whose sexual energies contribute to the kind of love God has for us and wants us to show for one another.

———

Recently on a retreat a young Jesuit told me of something that happened to him one day when he was spending his junior year of college in Ireland. He decided to go by himself on a walking tour to a small town south of Dublin called Brae. It turned out to be a rainy day. As he was walking a path along the sea, he noticed a pathway that led upward and felt an urge to follow it. He did so, and at least a couple of times began to doubt the wisdom of taking this path.

It was a relatively steep climb, and at one point, as he looked back, he realized that he would be in deep trouble if he slipped and fell. Each time he questioned himself, however, the same urge to go forward propelled him upward. When he got to the top, the sky suddenly cleared, the sun poured down, and he saw nothing but beauty wherever he looked. Then across a small valley he noticed a very large cross brightly illumined by the sun. He was overcome by a sense of being loved by God and began to cry. He has never forgotten that day, and he believes that God's Spirit moved him to take that path.

Has anything like that happened to you? Have you ever felt an urge that came unbidden and led you to do something that turned out to be a very pleasant surprise, perhaps even a great joy? Did you think that you were being moved by God? Perhaps you, too, have met God who is love in a surprising way.

Trust Unlimited

A woman I know told me the following story. She has been struggling with a difficult relationship where trust has been difficult to regain. When this happened, she had just returned from a trip.

> And then . . . I decided to finish the last chapter of a book I'd started in December. . . . Basically, it's about discovering God's dream for you, for your life, and it lays out some ideas about it. The last chapter is on trust, and serving, more or less—the idea that if we follow along doing what we know is the next good/right thing wherever we are right now, seeking to serve, exercising and strengthening our talents and gifts, our "mission" will be revealed to us by the Holy Spirit, step by step. And while we might not be able to see the whole of it at the outset, we have to trust that as we go along, God is guiding each next step. That's more or less what the chapter was about.
>
> So yesterday morning, there I was, standing at the kitchen sink, looking out the window to the house next door, thinking about trust, thinking about what my life's work is or will be now, thinking about how the greatest mission is love, and whatever that leads to with respect to my own work/writing, I may not yet know. . . . when all of a sudden I hear a dump truck pulling into the driveway of the house next door, right up beside my kitchen window. And I see the name of the company of the dump truck stenciled on the side door, right in front of my window—Trust Unlimited. How's that for God's way of speaking plain, and with a sense of humor!

And it's here again today because I need the reminder to loosen up, to loosen my grip, to enjoy, to delight in the world, in others, in myself, and to trust.

Have you ever experienced anything like that? Frederick Buechner wrote about a similar experience he had when he felt deeply distressed. He saw a license plate on a car that just said TRUST, and it changed the way he looked at life. A short time after his book with this story appeared, the person who had the license plate brought it to him, and he has it displayed prominently where it will remind him to trust God. On a trip to Switzerland, he saw, scratched on an old hay shed, *Gott heisst Lieben und Leben* (God is Love and Life). He follows up with these lines:

> *Trust* says the crumpled green license plate that hangs in my office. Trust what? Trust that it is worth scratching on a wall that God is Love and Life because, all appearances to the contrary notwithstanding, it may just be true. Trust that if God is anywhere, God is here, which means that there is no telling where God may turn up next—around what sudden bend of the path if you happen to have your eyes open, your wits about you, in what odd, small moments almost too foolish to tell.[5]

I think that I have only touched the surface of how God shows his love for us through other human beings and through seemingly chance events. I hope that this chapter has ignited your own imagination and creativity and given you other avenues to explore. No doubt as we continue this journey of discovery, we will hit upon more ways that our always-surprising God has communicated love for us.

4

Compassion—God's Love in Action

At least twice in recent weeks (the summer of 2018) there have been reports in the news of automobile crashes where bystanders have jumped in to save the driver just before the car was consumed by flames. In one instance, the driver was an elderly man who suddenly veered off a highway and crashed into some trees. Two or three bystanders rushed in as the flames started; they broke open the window of the car and dragged the man out just in time. These bystanders risked their lives to save a stranger. I thought of Jesus' story of the Good Samaritan.

The Good Samaritan

Just then a lawyer stood up to test Jesus. "Teacher," he said, "what must I do to inherit eternal life?" He said to him, "What is written in the law? What do you read there?" He answered, "You shall love the Lord your God with all your heart, and with all your soul, and with all your strength, and with all your mind; and your neighbor as yourself." And he said to him, "You have given the right answer; do this, and you will live."

But wanting to justify himself, he asked Jesus, "And who is my neighbor?" Jesus replied, "A man was going down from Jerusalem to Jericho, and fell into the hands of robbers, who stripped him, beat him, and went away, leaving him half dead. Now by chance a priest was going down that road; and when he saw him, he passed by on the other side. So likewise a Levite, when he came to the place and saw him, passed by on the other side. But a Samaritan while traveling came near him; and when he saw him, he was moved with pity. He went to him and bandaged his wounds, having poured oil and wine on them. Then he put him on his own animal, brought him to an inn, and took care of him. The next day he took out two denarii, gave them to the innkeeper, and said, 'Take care of him; and when I come back, I will repay you whatever more you spend.' Which of these three, do you think, was a neighbor to the man who fell into the hands of the robbers?" He said, "The one who showed him mercy." Jesus said to him, "Go and do likewise." (Luke 10:25–37)

This story is contained in Luke's larger story of Jesus' life, ministry, and death. As with the whole Gospel story, this story is designed to draw us into its orbit. We can imagine how the story unfolds, even adding details that Jesus omits. Three men see the mugged and wounded man, whom I presume is Jewish, by the side of the road.

I imagine that all three feel some stirring of feelings for this man and wonder if he is still alive and needs help. I even presume that all of them feel an urge to go to help him; they are human beings, made in the image of God, after all. But two do not follow up on this urge, this beginning of compassion. They are Jewish religious leaders, a priest and a Levite. Something keeps them from acting to help. The Samaritan, one of the enemies of Israel, "was moved with pity" and took action. He followed up on the urge to help a fellow human being in trouble. He took a chance that might have gotten him into deep trouble if the "wounded" man was only a plant to lure unsuspecting travelers toward a band of robbers, not an unknown danger on that road from Jerusalem to Jericho.

In this story, Luke uses the Greek word referring to guts to indicate the Samaritan's emotion upon seeing the wounded man. He is moved in his guts, literally. The NRSV translation I use says, "moved with pity," but the better translation, I believe, is "compassion." In the Hebrew Bible, this Greek word is used to translate the Hebrew word *rachamim*, a word that has resonances with the word for womb; it's the kind of love and concern a woman would have for her own child. In translations of the Hebrew Bible into English, the word *compassion* is most often used. The word *rachamim* is used to describe God when he is moved with compassion for his people and takes action to help them. So, in this Lukan story, the Samaritan *imitates God* by acting on the strong emotion of compassion to take the risk of helping a fellow human being in trouble.

I believe that all of us, because we are made in the image of God, are moved with compassion when we see someone in need. But not all of us act on this movement. I presume that there were bystanders at the accident of the elderly gentleman who did not act on their urge to compassion. Thank God, there were some who did act on the urge.

I hope that what you have just read has brought back to you memories of being moved by compassion yourself and of seeing others act with compassion toward you. Maybe you find yourself wanting to talk with Jesus about your own reactions of being the object of someone else's compassion or of having been stirred to do something to help someone who was in need.

Jesus Is Moved with Compassion

In the Gospels, Jesus is often depicted as being moved with this gut or womb love, this compassion. In Mark's Gospel it happens very early, near the end of the first chapter:

A leper came to him begging him, and kneeling he said to him, "If you choose, you can make me clean." Moved with pity, Jesus stretched out his hand and touched him, and said to him, "I do choose. Be made clean!" Immediately the leprosy left him, and he was made clean. After sternly warning him he sent him away at once, saying to him, "See that you say nothing to anyone; but go, show yourself to the priest, and offer for your cleansing what Moses commanded, as a testimony to them." But he went out and began to proclaim it freely, and to spread the word, so that Jesus could no longer go into a town openly, but stayed out in the country; and people came to him from every quarter. (Mark 1:40–45)

Did you notice "Moved with pity"? That's a translation of the same Greek word for "guts" often translated "compassion." So, here Jesus is moved as God is moved and risks himself as God does. Here Jesus risks getting the disease by touching the leper—and he definitely makes himself ritually unclean according to his own religion. This story can be taken as a metaphor of what God does in becoming a human being. God, in a sense, becomes contaminated by our sinfulness. As Paul writes, "For our sake he [the Father] made him [Jesus] to be sin who knew no sin, so that in him we might become the righteousness of God" (2 Corinthians 5:21).

A Jesuit Shows Compassion for Me

Years ago, when I was a young Jesuit studying theology before ordination, I was in a deep funk because of a betrayal by someone I thought of as a friend. Another Jesuit, Harold Bumpus, knocked at my door to talk with me about what had happened. Harry was someone who had rubbed me the wrong way for many years. I did not like him, and I presumed that he felt the same way about me. I was quite wrong about Harry. He had witnessed what happened and wanted to help me get over the hurt. In other words, Harry was moved with compassion and took the chance to talk with me. Harry and I became friends from that day until he died. At the time, I did not think of him as God's emissary, but in later years that's how I interpreted it. He was my Good Samaritan who was moved by compassion and took a chance to knock on my door and offer me his friendship.

Harry was an image of God for me, don't you think? Are you reminded of anything by this story? Have you yourself felt the urge that Harry felt and acted on it? Have you been the object of someone else's compassionate actions? Then you, too, know from experience how God, who is compassion itself, appears in human form, either through you or to you through others. You may want to talk with God the Father or with Jesus about your reactions and your stories. Go ahead and see how the conversation goes.

Acting Like the Priest and Levite

Perhaps, too, you recall times when you have felt the urge to compassion and have not acted on it. I have presumed that the priest and Levite were both moved by compassion and did not act on it. As I wrote this section, I thought of a few times when I did not act on the urge to show compassion. One time when a friend and I were coming out of the Boston subway to go to Symphony Hall, both of us noticed a woman trip just ahead of us. I was intent on getting to the concert on time and did nothing, but my friend went over to the woman to see if she needed any help.

Given my single-mindedness when I am headed someplace or have something to do, I presume that I have missed the boat of compassion many times, for which I am ashamed of myself. I hope, however, that reminding myself of these times will make me more like God in the future.

Can you remember a time when you failed to act on your feelings of compassion? If so, you have something else to talk over with God.

Acting Like the Good Samaritan

A man I know has been free of cancer for a few years but still sees his cancer doctor periodically. Recently when he and his wife were at the cancer clinic, a young couple with a small child were waiting. It turned out that the father was undergoing treatment for cancer. My friend felt a great burst of compassion for that family. He did not speak with the parents, but I felt certain, when he told me the story, that they must have felt some of that compassion wash over them as they waited for the father's treatment.

I recall what a Jesuit told me of his trips to the hospital with Jim McDavitt, SJ, who was being treated for a brain tumor, from which he eventually died. Jim always spoke warmly and compassionately with the other patients who were waiting for treatment. He brought the compassion of God into that waiting room, I'm sure. Maybe these stories will remind you of something in your own life that also brought you the compassion of God, or, indeed, when you were the compassion of God for someone else.

Stories from a Novel

Novels or other works of literature can also offer moments when you meet the God of compassion. In the late summer of 2018, I reread *Plainsong*, a novel by Kent Haruf about the people of Holt, a fictional small town in the high plains of Colorado. In one scene, Victoria Roubideaux, a high school senior who has become pregnant, sees an old country doctor for the first time since she found out she was pregnant. He is very gentle and kind to her. Near the end, having confirmed her pregnancy and determined that she wants to keep the baby, the doctor changes back into his suit coat and comes back to talk with Victoria. The following scene takes place.

> For the first time the girl released the hold on herself a little. Her eyes welled up. It was as if what she wanted to ask him was more important and more frightening than anything either one of them had said or done so far. She said, Is the baby all right? Would you tell me that?
>
> Oh, he said. Why yes. So far as I can tell, everything is fine. Didn't I make that clear? There is no reason why that should change, so long as you take care of yourself. I didn't mean to frighten you.
>
> She let herself cry silently just a little, while her shoulders slumped forward and her hair fell across her face. The old doctor reached up and took her hand and held it warmly between both of his hands for a moment and was quiet with her, simply looking into her face, serenely, grandfatherly, but not talking, treating her out of respect and kindness, out of his own long experience of patients in examination rooms.[6]

As I read it (and as I reread it during editing of this book), tears came to my eyes. In this novel we meet a doctor who imaged the compassion of God for this young girl in trouble. I don't know whether Kent Haruf had this theological thought in mind, but whether he did or not, he definitely loved this old doctor and Victoria, both products of his fertile imagination. I choose to believe that he was being guided by the Spirit of God in writing this novel and in producing this touching scene.

Just before I turned the lights out a few evenings later, I had read more of Haruf's novel and was touched by the shy but strong kindness shown by the two old brothers who had been asked to take Victoria in when her mother turned her out of the house. When I turned the lights out, I did what I usually do, a breathing prayer that begins by naming "Father, Son, and Holy Spirit" on the inbreath and ends on the outbreath usually with a request like "Take away my desire for control." This time I surprised myself by saying, and meaning, "I love You." Tears came to my eyes as I said this. I had been deeply touched by the unshowy but profound care shown by these characters in the novel that gave me hope for the human race. God's grace is everywhere.

Have you had any experiences like these either in real life or while reading a novel or short story? Perhaps reading this chapter will make you more attuned to the presence of our compassionate God everywhere.

A Moving News Story

As I finish this section (July 11, 2018), the whole world breathes a sigh of relief and joy with the news that the twelve young soccer players from Thailand and their coach have been successfully brought out of the flooded cave where they were marooned for two weeks. Their story held the attention and called out the compassion of people around the world, most of whom could do little but pray for the success of the rescue attempts.

When I heard that the last four boys and the coach had been successfully brought out, tears of joy filled my eyes and I had to tell others the news. I noticed that they, too, had tears in their eyes. I imagine that such tears were shed all over the world by people of every race, religion, and culture.

All of us wept because we were relieved and overjoyed. Those boys and their plight tugged at our hearts, hearts made in the image and likeness of God. For these two weeks, in spite of the continued wars and fighting, the clash of opinions and feelings that also had a place in our hearts, we were one in our concern for those boys; we were one in heart and mind, as God wants us to be all the time.

Mind you, all this was made possible because the Thai authorities mobilized the resources of that country and others, and eighteen heroic divers from Thailand, Australia, the United Kingdom, China, Denmark, and the United States risked their lives to save the boys. Indeed, one of the Thai divers did lose his life when his oxygen failed. The media, too, did its part to rivet the attention of the world to that tortuous cave in Thailand.

Perhaps it was the coming together of all these human beings, governmental leaders, media people, trained Navy Seals and other experts, ordinary people on the ground, and all of us throughout the world hoping and praying to God—all of us, I say, acting as images of God—that brought about what we all hoped for: the saving of these twelve boys and their coach.

The Thai Navy Seals in a Facebook posting afterward wrote, "We're not sure whether this is a miracle, a science, or what." I presume to say that it was a miracle of grace that included science, long training, expertise, and many other factors. I believe that the whole world witnessed, whether aware of it or not, God in action through the cooperation of millions of people made in God's image.

What do you think? How did you react to the events of those harrowing weeks when the twelve boys' and their coach's fate hung in the balance? Or are you remembering another event that demonstrated God's presence through the compassion of people? Do you want to talk to God about your reactions or anything else? Go ahead.

5

Daily Occurrences of "God with Us"

During Advent we sing the hymn "O Come, O Come, Emmanuel," whose refrain is "Rejoice, rejoice, Emmanuel shall come to thee, O Israel." The original Hebrew is *Immanu El* and means "God is with us." It appears in the book of the prophet Isaiah, who is trying to reassure King Ahaz of Israel that the two northern kingdoms attacking Israel will not succeed. When Ahaz refuses to ask for a sign, Isaiah tells him, "The Lord himself will give you a sign. Look, the young woman is with child and shall bear a son, and shall name him Immanuel" (Isaiah 7:14). God promises that he will be present to his people. Christians believe that Jesus is Immanuel, God with us.

God's Main Promise

Perhaps the main promise God makes is to be with us no matter what the circumstances. God does not promise that we will avoid all pain, all struggle, all sickness, all sorrow. Surely, God does not promise that we will never die. God does, however, promise to be with us, and that promise, I believe, can be a great comfort when we experience any of the things we so desperately want to avoid. (At times I have felt compassion for God as I imagine him saying, with some poignancy, "Am I not enough for you?")

When Isaiah spoke in God's name to King Ahaz, Israel was in a desperate situation. Not only were the northern kingdoms threatening, but the Babylonian empire posed an even greater danger. God promised that he would be with his people. The question they faced was whether they trusted in God's presence—that is, did they trust God to be enough for them?

Unfortunately for Israel, their leaders decided not to trust in God's presence and in the prophet's warning not to enter an alliance with Egypt. As a result, the Babylonians captured the city of Jerusalem, sacked it, destroyed the temple where God dwelt, and took into captivity a large number of the Jewish population. It was a disaster for the

Israelites, one that they overcame only about a half a century later through God's intervention.

God remained with the exiled Israelites, as we find out from Second Isaiah (chapters 40—55) and the prophet Ezekiel. Both these prophets wrote breathtakingly tender and marvelously creative predictions of how God would continue to be with this sinful and exiled people. Let me give you two examples.

Second Isaiah, chapters 40—55, was written during the Babylonian exile to a people who were beaten down, often enslaved, and far from their beloved homeland. Moreover, they knew that they or their leaders had brought the disaster on themselves by not heeding God's word and trusting in God's presence. Yet Second Isaiah opens with these tender words so familiar from the opening lines of Handel's *Messiah*:

> Comfort, O comfort my people,
>   says your God.
> Speak tenderly to Jerusalem,
>   and cry to her
> that she has served her term,
>   that her penalty is paid,
> that she has received from the LORD's hand
>   double for all her sins.
>
> —Isaiah 40:1–2

This deeply troubled people must have experienced great consolation when they first heard these words. To this day the same comfort comes over people in darkness, whatever the cause, who hear these words as directed to them.

In chapter 3 I cited part of Isaiah 43. You might want to look at that again. This passage repeats a recurring theme of the Bible, namely, that God is with the Israelites. This promise still holds. God never reneges on his promises. Even when it seems as though God has left the covenanted people of Israel, it becomes clear that God has not and never will renege.

The presence of Jesus of Nazareth in our world is the final proof that God will never leave us, that God is with us forever. Now God is one of us, bone of our bone, and flesh of our flesh. In Jesus, God suffered even death on a Roman cross, killed by human hands. Even that terrible act did not cause God to give up on us. Indeed, Jesus' risen body, still bearing the wounds of the Crucifixion, is forever a part of who God is, and that body, like all bodies, has ties to the whole created universe. God is that much in love with us and with the whole of creation. God is that much *with* us. Immanuel indeed!

Over the centuries, many people have been heartened by reading and applying these prophecies to themselves. They have found solace in dark times.

Can you remember such times, when you were encouraged by the knowledge—or the tangible sense—of God with you? Spend a few moments pondering those memories.

"From One Human to Another, What's Up?"

This story is from "Metropolitan Diary" a weekly feature of the *New York Times*. People from the metropolitan New York area send in notices of events that happened to them. Molly Burdick's story appeared in the *The New York Times* for February 4, 2019.

Dear Diary: I had an appointment to see an apartment and, according to Google Maps, had left exactly enough time to get there from work.

Of course, I got there late and missed the appointment completely when the real estate agent had to go home.

I was in the Barclays Center subway station. I began to feel overwhelmed by the prospect of trying to find a permanent place to live. I started to cry.

The R wasn't coming, so I decided to walk to Fulton Street to get the G. I was still crying when I walked onto the platform at the station there.

A woman smiled at me. Embarrassed, I averted my eyes and brushed past her.

"Are you O.K?" I heard her ask.

She patted the seat next to her.

"From one human to another," she said. "What's up?"

I sat down beside her and, still crying, began to explain everything. We talked until, at some point, I started to laugh.

When the train arrived, we got on together. And then we got off at the same stop. It turned out that she had lived in my neighborhood for 15 years.

Molly Burdick

The woman who reached out to Molly made my point when she said, "From one human to another, what's up?" She was a human being, an image of God, and thus a sign of God's presence for Molly.

"You're a Great Tonic for Your Mother"

Sr. Lisette Michaud left her family at thirteen to participate in her congregation's juniorate high school program. Some years later, after her profession, she was visiting her elderly parents. Just before she left, her father put his arms on her shoulders and with deep feeling said, "Lisette, you are a great tonic for your mother." She knew immediately that he was also speaking for himself. This exchange gave Sister

Lisette great consolation and a dose of self-confidence. Her father was Emmanuel for her.

Emmanuel

Do you remember the story of the mother and her youngest son, Michael, from chapter 3? Here is the mother's reflection on the ordeal she and her husband went through when their first child was born with clubfeet.

Our oldest son, Jason, was born with severe bilateral clubfeet. This condition, if left untreated, would prevent him from walking. The treatment is very intense and must happen immediately. So, ten days after he was born, we brought him to begin a lengthy process of treatment. The early stages of his treatment involved serial, full leg casting on both legs. The doctor would slowly and methodically manipulate each foot to a new position and cast it from his toes to his diaper. Our son had this done for nine consecutive weeks. As a new mom, it was a very overwhelming and painful experience to have to accompany Jason to these treatments.

In my heart, I knew these treatments were helping his condition. However, not to be able to do anything to stop his discomfort and his crying was awful. From the moment we walked into the hospital Jason would scream bloody murder each week! The doctors and nurses started to call him "Killer Jason" because of his shrill screams. But, each week we would have to return to the hospital and undergo this process.

Each week as we walked into the hospital, my prayer was the same, "Please God, accompany me. Please God, help me to help Jason. Please God, help me to accept whatever news the doctors deliver. Please God, help me to know, to see, to feel, and to experience You. Please God, help me to trust that You are with me." My desire was to trust the all loving and all present God that I knew. But the reality of the situation and my fear were causing me to doubt whether God was truly with me. Each week I prayed as I carried Jason into the casting room and tried to trust God.

As his treatment continued, I became aware of a little boy, who also had clubfeet, who was sitting in the casting room waiting for his treatment after my son's. He was a seven-year-old from Haiti who did not speak English and was born with the same condition as my son. He had not received any treatment for his clubfeet and was in a wheelchair, receiving whatever treatment they could give him at this point. This little boy would simply sit on the table next to us. I would look at him, and he would smile. Jason would scream and wave his arms and kick his legs and do anything to make this treatment stop. Yet this little boy from Haiti would simply smile, not bothered by the screaming and the noise, and thus he would offer me a moment of comfort and relief. I soon learned that this little boy's name was Emmanuel, God with us. God was with me, was with us, in our time of darkness, our time of fear, our time of uncertainty.

Jason is now ten years old and has continued to receive treatment for his clubfeet. He has endured two surgeries, which left him immobile for lengthy periods of time. And the memory of Emmanuel, this little seven-year-old boy from Haiti, continues to offer me comfort and hope and serves as a beautiful reminder of God's abiding presence in times of darkness, fear, uncertainty, and doubt.

This mother found God's presence in that seven-year-old Haitian boy who met her look every time with a smile. But her son met God, again whether he knows it or not, in the suffering love of his mother and father through those painful years. And we who read this story and let it touch our hearts also experience God's presence.

Does this story remind you of something similar you have undergone or witnessed? When have you seen God's presence in those who have accompanied you or loved ones through difficult times? Perhaps you want to talk to God about what we have just considered.

"I Would Go to the Darkest Place to Be with You"

Another story: A mother was undergoing breast cancer treatments. One day when she came home from a treatment, she found a picture painted by her ten-year-old daughter. To grasp the full meaning of the picture, you need to know that the daughter had a very deep fear of dark places. The picture is kind of dim and foggy looking. It's night because there are faint stars and a moon in the sky over a house. Written at the top of the picture is the word *Mom*, and beside the house, "I would go to the darkest place to be with you."

You can imagine how that picture flooded her mother with happiness despite what she was going through. That ten-year-old girl was God's comforting presence for her mother that day. If the story touches you, as it did me, then you, too, have met the comforting presence of God through this ten-year-old girl.

God in Our Dark Places

Scripture sometimes brings a sense of God's comforting presence in the darkness that can envelop our lives. In *Speaking of Faith: Why Religion Matters—and How to Talk About It*, Krista Tippett recounts what happened in a class on the New Testament that she took at Yale Divinity

School. Her teacher was Leander Keck, whose wife of many years was in the late stages of Alzheimer's disease. Keck carried the burden quietly but publicly. At the end of the year he read from Revelation 7, a reading that Tippett will never forget. She quotes the passage Keck read:

> They shall hunger no more, neither thirst any more;
> The sun shall not strike them, nor any
>   scorching heat.
> For the Lamb in the midst of the throne will be their
>   shepherd,
> And he will guide them to springs of living water;
> And God will wipe away every tear from their eyes.
>
>   —Revelation 7:16–17

Tippett goes on:

> As he read this to us, tears filled his eyes. All of us knew he was thinking of his wife and the terrible grief of the last chapter of their life together. He was cleaving to that promise tucked between Revelation's demons and reckonings and battles: of a tender ultimate encounter with God when the sadness will be gathered up, the defects mended, the tears wiped away. We rose to our feet and applauded him and tears pricked our eyes as well and so did the promise in those lines. You could see this as selective reading, wishful thinking. But looking at the person of Leander Keck, I believed it with all my heart.[7]

Perhaps you, too, are moved by this man's story and the passage he read. We have met God and found him kind and merciful and compassionate. If you are so moved, talk with God about your reactions.

Elie Wiesel and the Holocaust

Six million or more Jews were killed in the Nazi death camps before and during the Second World War. Many gypsies and homosexuals were also exterminated. The question raised for many by these horrors was, "Where was God?" There is no easy answer to this question. Some survivors felt the presence of God in the camps; others lost whatever faith in God they had. I was deeply moved by reading Elie Wiesel's conversation with Krista Tippett. Tippett asked Wiesel to read a section of his memoir in which he professed his loss of faith in the camps. Wiesel asked her to read it to him. Here is what she read:

> Never shall I forget that night, the first night in camp, which has turned my life into one long night, seven times cursed and seven times sealed. Never shall I forget that smoke. Never shall I forget the little faces of the children, whose bodies I saw turned into wreaths of smoke beneath a silent blue sky.
>
> Never shall I forget those flames which consumed my faith forever.

Never shall I forget that nocturnal silence which deprived me, for all eternity, of the desire to live. Never shall I forget those moments which murdered my God and my soul and turned my dreams to dust. Never shall I forget these things, even if I am condemned to live as long as God Himself. Never.

When she finished reading, Tippett asked Wiesel "What happened after that . . . after you lost your faith forever?"

Wiesel responded, "What happened after is in the book. . . . I went on praying." Then he gave Tippett (and us) the following gift of that prayer.

I no longer ask You for either happiness or paradise; all I ask of You is to listen and let me be aware of Your listening.

I no longer ask You to resolve my questions, only to receive them and make them part of You.

I no longer ask You for either rest or wisdom, I only ask You not to close me to gratitude, be it of the most trivial kind, or to surprise and friendship. Love? Love is not Yours to give.

As for my enemies, I do not ask You to punish them or even to enlighten them; I only ask You not to lend them Your mask and Your powers. If You must relinquish one or the other, give them Your powers. But not Your countenance.

They are modest, my requests, and humble. I ask You what I might ask a stranger met by chance at twilight in a barren land.

I ask you, God of Abraham, Isaac, and Jacob, to enable me to pronounce these words without betraying the child that transmitted them to me: God of Abraham, Isaac, and Jacob, enable me to forgive You and enable the child I once was to forgive me too.

I no longer ask You for the life of that child, nor even for his faith. I only beg You to listen to him and act in such a way that You and I can listen to him together.[8]

When I first read these prayers, the horror of the Holocaust hit home to me again. It occurred to me, not for the first time, that the tears I shed at that moment were a very pale reflection of God's reactions to the horror of the Holocaust and to other horrors perpetrated by us humans. But I also thanked God for being Elie Wiesel's God, for being the God of Abraham, Isaac, and Jacob, who listened to him and comforted him despite the horror. I don't understand everything that Wiesel prays for in this prayer; all I know is that I was in the presence of someone who, in spite of all that he and his people had suffered, still found some solace in God. I include this prayer here in the hope that it will give you some sense of how to talk honestly to God in times of great suffering and sorrow. Emmanuel, indeed.

My reaction to Elie Wiesel's prayer reminded me of a similar reaction at the end of the movie *Born into Brothels*, which I saw some years ago. That film is about children of the women living in the Calcutta brothels and what the children did with cameras given by the filmmaker. The children's pictures were shown at an international exhibition in Brussels. The movie also showed the poverty and suffering of all the children and the loss of hope of some. At the end I sobbed uncontrollably for a few moments. On reflection, I felt that I had sensed some of God's compassion and presence to those children and all the poor children of the world.

When have you sensed God's presence through the sorrow and compassion it inspired?

Anger and Sorrow Because of the Abuse Crisis in the Church

God showed himself to Marsha (a pseudonym), who was deeply grieved and angered by the latest news of the sexual abuse crisis in the Roman Catholic Church. On the anniversary of the death of her son (who died a tragically early death), his widow, who was born in Brazil, offered to have a memorial Mass at her Brazilian parish in

Massachusetts. The widow has remarried and now has three more children. At the church, two of the younger children started yelling "Papa! Papa!" when they saw the priest enter the church. The priest, who hails from Brazil, opened his arms wide, spreading the chasuble out to embrace the kids. They ran into his arms, and he embraced them and gently ushered them back to their mother and grandparents. During the Mass, the priest twice mentioned Marsha's son's name and, as he did so, looked directly over at her and her husband. Marsha understood the gestures of this priest toward her grandchildren and her as God's way of easing her grief and anger.

At some point during this time she asked God directly how God reacts to this scandal and felt such a deep sadness and hurt that it was almost too much to bear. She believes that this reaction was God's answer to her question. Around the same time, at a Sunday liturgy, another priest spoke movingly of his own grief and anger at what was revealed. Marsha took this as another indication of how God reacts and also how God eases the grief of a congregation through someone acting in God's image and likeness. The closing hymn at that same liturgy was "Christ, Be Our Light" by Bernadette Farrell whose refrain is "Christ, be our light!/

Shine in our hearts/ Shine through the darkness./ Christ, be our light!/ Shine in Your church gathered today."

As she sang with the congregation, tears poured down Marsha's cheeks. Through this song God was telling her that Christ was the light of the world and of the church no matter what, and that she and all her fellow Christians were called to be light for the world by allowing Christ's light to shine in their hearts. Despite her anger and grief at the scandal of the abuse and its cover-up, she was determined to be a light for the little part of the world she inhabits.

A few weeks later she met an older priest in her parish with a hearty "How are you, Fr. X?" He, quite unexpectedly and out of character, threw his arms around her and thanked her. In this case Marsha became, it seems, an image of God for this priest.

Finally, she received an e-mail from the pastor of a church that is not hers, but on whose mailing list she is. This e-mail was a letter to all his parishioners expressing sorrow for what has happened in the church and sharing their sadness, grief, and anger. Again, she felt that God was consoling her through this honest priest.

Another woman I know wrote me the following:

While I was praying over the story of the Prodigal Son, I was filled with anger at how the hierarchical church has squandered our inheritance. The anger lingered with me for some time but was transformed into a renewed experience of God's abundant love and forgiveness because of my grandchild. I was waiting for her to come out the door of her preschool when the doors burst open and out she ran, jumping and shrieking my name when she saw me and ran to me. She threw her arms around my legs, holding on tight, then took my hand as she skipped and jumped to the car for the ride home. For me it was a vivid experience of God's love and acceptance of all of us, of forgiveness, of "second chances," and I was able to let go of the anger and pray for forgiveness of the Church and myself.

These stories of reactions to the scandal of sexual abuse and its cover-up may now become an instance of God's compassionate presence to you as you read them. Maybe they speak to your anger and grief and assure you of God's comforting presence with you and with all of us. If so moved, you might have a conversation with God about your own reactions.

It may be that after all your prayers of anger and anguish, you still feel betrayed and angry at the church. That can be painful indeed, but I would suggest that you not give up on expressing to God how you feel. One thought that might help: What if your sense of betrayal and anger reflects something of how God reacts to the way things are being done in the church?

Unexpected Good Samaritans

Sometimes the presence of God comes through someone from whom you would not expect it. You may recall my experience with Harold Bumpus from chapter 4. When I was in a low state, someone I never expected became the compassionate presence of God for me.

The train conductor in the following story was an unexpected Good Samaritan. *The New York Times'* "Metropolitan Diary" on Monday, October 1, 2018, had this moving story:

Dear Diary:

Scene: A weekday morning at rush hour aboard a Manhattan-bound Long Island Rail Road train car. A boy who looks about 13 asks the conductor when he should transfer at Jamaica to the Atlantic Terminal connection to Brooklyn.

With an empathetic look on his face, the conductor says the train is running express and will not stop in Jamaica.

I am sitting three rows away. I can feel the panic wash over the boy.

Not understanding, he asks again how to transfer at Jamaica.

Speaking with care and patience, the conductor gives the directions to Atlantic Terminal from Penn Station [the destination of this train] until, finally, the boy seems to understand.

About 15 minutes later, the train approaches the Jamaica station. The conductor returns to our car and gestures for the boy.

The train slows to a stop. The doors open for a moment, and the boy gets off to make his transfer. As he steps onto the platform, the doors close and the train continues on its way into Manhattan. The conductor smiles with satisfaction.

Stacey Ascher

Isn't that an amazing instance of someone being the compassionate presence of God? I don't know whether the writer or anyone who watched this event thought of someone being an image of our compassionate God, but for me it became an experience of meeting God in people of everyday life. The interesting thing is that, even if no one but I experienced God's presence at the time of the event or in reading or hearing the story, God was still present, working God's magic. And now the story still has a chance to reveal God's compassionate presence for you, dear reader, as it did for me. Perhaps, too, it reminds you of something that happened to you. If so, and if you did not think of God at the time, you have a chance to do so now.

These stories may remind you of a time or times when you were feeling down in the dumps and someone or something picked up your spirits. I hope that you will see, at least at this time, if not then, that these experiences were God's way of showing his steadfast presence and desire to console you. "Rejoice, Rejoice, Emmanuel will come to thee, O Israel."

6

Kindness and Mercy: Sure Signs of God

In the book of Exodus Moses begs God "Show me your glory, I pray" (Exodus 33:18). God agrees but tells him that he cannot see his face, only his back. Here is the description of God's revelation:

> The LORD descended in the cloud and stood with him there, and proclaimed the name, "The LORD." The LORD passed before him, and proclaimed,
> "The LORD, the LORD,
> a God merciful and gracious,
> slow to anger,
> and abounding in steadfast love and faithfulness,
> keeping steadfast love for the thousandth generation,
> forgiving iniquity and transgression and sin."
> —Exodus 34:5–7a

This revelation seems to have been etched in the memories of the Israelites because parts of it are often repeated (with some variations) in the Hebrew Bible. In this passage, God repeats the name *Yahweh*, given to Moses during his vision at the burning bush. In the New Revised Standard Version, the name is translated and printed "The LORD." God gives us a self-description as "merciful and gracious, slow to anger, and abounding in steadfast love and faithfulness, forgiving iniquity and transgression and sin," the lines from this passage that are most often quoted in other parts of the Bible. The words translated as "steadfast love" and "faithfulness" are associated with the covenant that God makes with the Israelites. In this chapter I would like to focus on God's kindness or graciousness and forgiveness and how we experience and mirror these traits of God, often in surprising ways.

Throughout their history the Israelites continually betrayed their covenant with God, often eliciting God's anger. But as I mentioned earlier, that anger was always overridden by kindness and mercy. In fact, this revelation to Moses was occasioned by God's red-hot anger at the Israelites for persuading Aaron, Moses' brother, to make a golden calf to worship while Moses was on Mount Sinai receiving the Ten Commandments. God's anger was assuaged only by Moses' pleas. Every time the Israelites fall,

God is ready to forgive them and take them back into the covenant. If you read the Old Testament, you will note how often the Israelites are depicted as fickle and unfaithful, provoking God to wrath, only to find that God was once again ready to forgive them. They are like us in this regard.

Biblical Examples of God's Kindness and Mercy

After the Israelites returned to the land of Israel from exile in Babylon and had begun to rebuild a life in the Promised Land, the book of Nehemiah records a prayer by Ezra that harks back to the vision of Moses. Here is part of that prayer:

> But they and our ancestors acted presumptuously and stiffened their necks and did not obey your commandments; they refused to obey, and were not mindful of the wonders that you performed among them; but they stiffened their necks and determined to return to their slavery in Egypt. But you are a God ready to forgive, gracious and merciful, slow to anger and abounding in steadfast love, and you did not forsake them. (Nehemiah 9:16–17)

One more example from the Hebrew Bible will again bring out how much love and kindness win out in God over anger, this one from the prophet Hosea. This book contains

a series of expressions of God's tender love for Israel followed by great anger at their fickleness and infidelity. Just
take a look at chapter 11, which begins with these tender lines:

> When Israel was a child, I loved him,
>   and out of Egypt I called my son.
> The more I called them,
>   the more they went from me;
> . . . offering incense to idols.
>
> —Hosea 11:1–2

God goes on to talk about how he nurtured Israel but then
leaves them to their folly and destruction. However, once
again God's immense kindness and mercy take over, and we
hear the following words:

> How can I give you up, Ephraim?
>   How can I hand you over, O Israel?
> . . . .
> My heart recoils within me;
>   my compassion grows warm and tender.
> I will not execute my fierce anger;
>   I will not again destroy Ephraim;
> for I am God and no mortal,
>   the Holy One in your midst,
>   and I will not come in wrath.
>
> —Hosea 11:8–9

Jesus knew of this tradition of the great kindness and mercy of God. Perhaps this is why he ate with tax collectors and sinners, to show by action who God is. Luke gives us an example in chapter 15 of that Gospel, which begins, "Now all the tax collectors and sinners were coming near to listen to him. And the Pharisees and the scribes were grumbling and saying, 'This fellow welcomes sinners and eats with them'" (Luke 15:1–2). Jesus replies with three parables: the lost sheep, the lost coin, and the prodigal son, each one of which tells the Pharisees and scribes and their listeners that God is a God of overabundant kindness and mercy.

The parable of the prodigal son tells the story of a father who is badly treated by his youngest son. The father gives this wastrel his inheritance, which he proceeds to throw away on dissolute living to the point that he wants to eat what the pigs eat. Having hit rock bottom, he decides to go back to his father, ask his forgiveness, and offer to work as one of the father's servants. The father, who would be expected to beat and/or throw out this wayward son, has been waiting for him all this time, "saw him and was filled with compassion; he ran and put his arms around him and kissed him" (Luke 15:20). Then he threw a party for him because "he was lost and is found!" (v. 24). That's who God is, Jesus tells his opponents.

God's Forgiving Presence through Others

Perhaps you can remember a time when you experienced the kindness and mercy of God. Maybe it was during a high school or college retreat or when you confessed your sins in the sacrament of reconciliation. If so, then you know some of what the prodigal son experienced in that story Jesus told.

But maybe you experienced something similar when you were forgiven by a parent or sibling or friend after you had hurt that person badly. Take some time to look back over your past experiences to see if you remember such an event. Events such as these are examples of how human beings act as the image of God. God is clearly present at these moments. Perhaps, too, you can remember a time when you yourself forgave someone who had gravely hurt you. If so, then you know from experience what it is like to be an image of the God who is so generous in kindness and mercy to us all.

I remember that in a fit of anger once I hurt a close friend very deeply. I said things that seemed to me unforgivable, yet this friend not only forgave me when I expressed my remorse but has remained a friend to this day. She has been, for me, the presence of God for sure. The only way I can explain this kind of forgiving love is to understand that it was God working overtime, as it were, in my friend's heart. Maybe you recall something similar. If you do, then we both have much for which to be grateful to God and to our friend.

Parents Forgive an Errant Son

In *An Invitation to Love* I cited a story told by Nick Genovese, a young intern at the Jesuit magazine *America*. He was terribly distraught at the election of Donald Trump as president and angry at his parents who had voted for Mr. Trump. In a fit of pique, he wrote a blog expressing his anger at his parents without first talking with them, and posted it on Facebook.

He thought of calling them to express his remorse, but Facebook got to them first. He got a call from his parents. His mother's opening line was to say that she and his father had read the article and wanted to know how he was. He started to express his remorse. Her response was, "I love you and am so proud that you have matured to develop a different perspective than your father and I." His father chimed in, "Amazing article, buddy. You know I'm your number one fan, Nicholas."

Isn't that a great example of kindness and mercy? Nick Genovese's parents were for him a sacramental sign of God's great love and forgiveness as he makes clear in the following comment:

> My mom and dad did not care what thousands of readers and hundreds of commenters thought about them. They only wanted to tell me that no matter what I wrote or other people said, I am their beloved son.
>
> And so it is with God. The ground of our hope is knowing that even when we turn away, God is infinitely in love with us, always reaching out to us.[9]

A Man Imprisoned for Thirty-two Years for a Crime He Did Not Commit

When Darrell Jones, the ex-prisoner I mentioned in chapter 2, was freed from prison just before Christmas of 2017, he came to live in my Jesuit community for the first ten months of his freedom. A few days after his arrival Darrell, his sister, his cousin, and some of us Jesuits were watching a program on TV that featured an interview with Darrell. During a break Darrell turned to me and Bill Russell, SJ, and asked us, with tears in his eyes, to pray for him to be able to forgive one or two of the people responsible for his imprisonment, especially a detective who lied under oath at his trial. Bill and I have never forgotten this. Darrell would be the last one to think of himself as an image of God, but he certainly was that for us. He wants to be an image of our kind and merciful God.

A Young Girl Paralyzed for Life Forgives the Shooter

I suspect that forgiveness has effects on everyone who has been forgiven, but sometimes we come across instances of great transformation. One of these occurred in Boston a few years ago. In 2003, three-year-old Kai Leigh Harriott was hit by a stray bullet which left her paralyzed from the waist down. The young man who did the shooting, Anthony Warren, was caught and convicted. At his sentencing hearing in 2006, Kai Leigh publicly forgave Anthony.

This young man was imprisoned for his actions that awful day, but his life was changed by the forgiveness. A year later he sent a videotaped apology to Kai Leigh in which he thanked her and her mother and family for their forgiveness. He continued, "I want to apologize to my community. I just appreciate the opportunity you gave me." In prison Anthony came under the influence of Darrell Jones and joined in various works of outreach to the community from which he came. He finished his sentence and is now a useful working citizen.

Whenever you begin to think that evil is winning in this world (a constant temptation these days), remember this story. A young girl, severely and permanently wounded, showed the man who caused her disability the real face of God. That forgiveness changed him for the better. Moreover, her forgiving act shows all those who hear the story how powerful being an image of God can be in this world. (By the way, Kai Leigh graduated from Newton Country Day School in 2018 and still feels strongly about the need for and power of forgiveness.)

A Mother Comforts Her Son

Here is a story told to me by a young Jesuit. It's another example of God's kindness and mercy shown by one of his human images. The Jesuit wrote it out for me:

> One crucial moment from my past that touches upon different elements of grief and loss recently resurfaced during a faith-sharing session I had with some brother Jesuits in which we were reflecting on how we have been touched by moments of "annunciation" from God. I recalled a crucial moment from when I was twelve years old at my great-grandmother's funeral.
>
> Some family background information will help elucidate the moment. My grandfather (on my mother's side) died when my mom was nine years old. According

to my mom, over the next ten years my grandmother responded to this loss in her life through harshly disciplining her children and never really supporting or loving them in very positive ways. My grandmother fell in love with and married a man who loved her but not her children. Eventually he forced her to choose between him and them. Sadly, she chose him over them.

This "fundamental" choice, if you will, really took a toll on my mom and uncles, and it elicited resentment in my extended family. My mom tells me that in the years following she would reach out to her mother and husband with the hope of reconciliation. The rest of her family was not interested in reconciliation. Therefore, as I reflect on my memory of her when I was growing up, I never really considered her my grandmother. I knew in my head she was my grandmother in name and biological terms. It never felt like she was my grandmother in the ways that other classmates and friends had described theirs.

All this background information became clearer and sobering to me at my great-grandmother's funeral. After the funeral ended, my extended family hosted everybody at my great-aunt's home. I remember pulling up to the house, getting out of the car, and seeing my grandmother, her (now) husband, and their older daughter coming toward us in a defiant manner. My grandmother was putting up a fight and shouting at the top of her lungs, "Nana would've wanted me to be here! We have every right to be here!" I was, of course, startled by the yelling and hostility. I remember my mom being very calm during this time. She simply responded to her mother, "You know, over the years we've offered reconciliation over and over again, and you've refused it every time. I don't know what else to say to you." And my grandmother, her husband, and their daughter stomped off, shouting that this whole thing was "unbelievable!"

At that moment, I felt a rush of fear and confusion at the whole situation. Sobbing profusely, I ran into the house—past all the family members and guests—straight to my great-aunt's room, which was always designated as the room where the kids could play. For me, it was the place I felt most comfortable, at ease, and safe. I sat down against the wall and continued to sob. Soon my mom came into the room, sat down next to me, and began to hold me, gently rocking me back and forth while stroking my hair. She apologized for my having to witness that whole interaction. Then she asked me if I was okay.

I had calmed down a little at this point but shook my head. She responded very lovingly, "What's the matter? You can tell me." At this point the tears flowed out once again, and I told her that I was afraid.

"Of what, honey?"

"Are you going to leave Liz and me, like your mom did with you?"

My mom got very emotional. Tears welled up in her eyes, and she said, "Oh, sweetie . . . no, I will never leave you and Liz. Many children want to grow up and be like their parents. But I don't want to be like my mother. I love you two so much. . . . I won't leave you no matter what."

I instantly felt a sense of relief, peace, and calm. That burst of love made me feel secure and able to move forward in greater trust.

I sobbed as I shared this moment with my brother Jesuits, which I was not expecting to do. (I actually had another moment in mind to share with them.) Upon further reflection, although I was not able to name it at the time, I do believe that moment was an instance of God's outpouring of deep love for me, an "annunciation of love" that has been resounding in my heart for many years.

Does this story touch you as it did me? Perhaps it reminds you of a time in your own life when God showed kindness and mercy through another, or when you were God's image of such kindness and mercy. You can talk with God about your feelings and your other reactions.

Uncommon Forgiveness in Rwanda

Rwanda has become a recent example of the power of hatred and evil in our world. The images of the heaped-up skulls are imprinted on our imaginations as reminders of the genocide attempted by Hutus against Tutsis and their defenders in that country twenty-five years ago. Those images join, for many of us older people, those of the atrocities perpetrated by the Nazis against the Jews during Hitler's years as dictator of Germany. These Rwandan horrors, however, cannot be allowed the last word because there are any number of remarkable stories of forgiveness and healing that give the last word to love and to God. Just one such story will suffice, and it is a remarkable one.

The Jesuit priest Marcel Uwineza lost his parents and some of his siblings in the Rwandan genocide. In *America* he wrote:

> Over the last 20 years, God has led me through a school of forgiveness. One day I met one of the killers of my brothers and sister. Upon seeing me, he came toward me. I thought he was coming to kill me too. But I could not believe what happened. As if in a movie, he knelt before me and asked me to forgive him. After a time of confusion, asking myself what was happening, and by a force which I could not describe, I took him, embraced him and said: "I forgive you; the Lord has been good to me." Ever since that moment, I have felt free.
>
> I have realized that forgiveness heals the forgiver even more than the forgiven. My wounds have been able to heal others. I later found myself desiring to give the gift of my very self to the Lord as a Jesuit.[10]

Isn't that a marvelous account of someone being an image of God? I hope you noticed that he was moved "by a force" he could not describe. The Spirit of God was working overtime, as it were, to move him to such generous mercy. If you recall something like this that happened to you, you can talk with God about it and thank him.

Mister Rogers, a Sign of God's Kindness and Mercy on TV

Over a year ago, millions of Americans flocked to the documentary film *Won't You Be My Neighbor?* about Fred Rogers's show on public TV. Mister Rogers was a minister who for more than thirty years entertained children and adults with his folksy humor, gentle kindness, and radical goodness and truthfulness. For example, during the time of civil strife over the rights of African Americans, when black children were being thrown out of public swimming pools, Rogers invited an African American character on the show to join him as he was cooling his feet in a tub. David Brooks, in an op-ed piece in *The New York Times*, put it this way:

There's nothing obviously moving here, yet the audience is moved: sniffling, wiping the moisture from their cheeks. The power is in Rogers' radical kindness at a time when public kindness is scarce. It's as if the pressure of living in a time such as ours gets released in that theater as we're reminded that, oh yes, that's how people can be.[11]

Maybe you saw the documentary. If so, did you think that you were in the presence of an image of God? Rather amazing, isn't it, that Mr. Rogers was able to touch so many lives over so many years just by being true to his own belief in the presence of God. He was a realist for those of us who believe in God. People can be images of God because of the presence of the Spirit of God moving all of us in that direction.

7

Joy and Loveliness: God's Trademarks

Have you ever thought of how much joy there must be in God? This might sound unusual—after all, we don't hear much about God's joy in church or anywhere else, do we? In this chapter I would like to explore this idea and ask you to recall times when you have been "surprised by joy" and perhaps missed how suffused by the presence of God such times were.

God Delights in Creating

At the very beginning of the Bible we catch a glimpse of God's delight in the world he is creating: "Then God said, 'Let there be light;' and there was light. And God saw that the light was good" (Genesis 1:3–4). Five more times in the next few verses we read, "And God saw that it was good" (verses 10, 12, 18, 21, 25). After the creation of human beings and the completion of the creation story we read, "God saw everything that he had made, and indeed, it was very good" (1:31). Clearly the writer of this creation story felt that God was delighted with the created world.

The writer of the book of Proverbs had the same intuition, as we see in these lines extolling the role of wisdom in creation. Wisdom herself is speaking:

> The LORD created me at the beginning of his work,
>> the first of his acts of long ago.
> Ages ago I was set up,
>> at the first, before the beginning of the earth.
> When there were no depths I was brought forth,
>> when there were no springs abounding with water.
> Before the mountains had been shaped,
>> before the hills, I was brought forth—
> when he had not yet made earth and fields,
>> or the world's first bits of soil.
> When he established the heavens, I was there,
>> when he drew a circle on the face of the deep,
> when he made firm the skies above,
>> when he established the fountains of the deep,
> when he assigned to the sea its limit,
>> so that the waters might not transgress his
>>> command,
> when he marked out the foundations of the earth,
>> then I was beside him, like a master worker;

and I was daily his delight,
>   rejoicing before him always,
> rejoicing in his inhabited world
>>   and delighting in the human race.

>   —Proverbs 8:21–31

Can you imagine, as this author did, God having a great time creating and delighting in the results of his work, which includes us humans? If so, what might you say to God in response?

There are numerous texts in the Bible that indicate God's delight, especially delight in the Israelites. Here are a couple: Psalm 37:23; Psalm 149:4. Luke's Gospel gives us an example of Jesus exulting with delight to his Father after listening to the reports of what his disciples had experienced on a missionary trip:

> At that same hour Jesus rejoiced in the Holy Spirit and said, "I thank you, Father, Lord of heaven and earth, because you have hidden these things from the wise and the intelligent and have revealed them to infants; yes, Father, for such was your gracious will. All things have been handed over to me by my Father; and no one knows who the Son is except the Father, or who the Father is except the Son and anyone to whom the Son chooses to reveal him."
>
> Then turning to the disciples, Jesus said to them privately, "Blessed are the eyes that see what you see! For

I tell you that many prophets and kings desired to see what you see, but did not see it, and to hear what you hear, but did not hear it." (Luke 10:21–24)

Jesus must have believed that his Father would be delighted to hear about his own delight at what the disciples reported. So, despite what we may have thought about God, let's take it for granted that God, in some mysterious fashion, delights in us, enjoys us, at least at times. Now the question for us is, Do we experience God's joy in our daily lives?

The Beauties of Nature

I had dinner recently with Sr. Ligita Ryliskyte from Lithuania, who is studying theology at Boston College. She and some of her immediate family had visited several of the most beautiful national parks in the United States. She was eager to show me some of her photos of Bryce Canyon and Antelope Canyon, places I had never seen. As I looked at the pictures, I was stunned by the beauty she had captured on film and reminded of times when I had been bowled over by the beauties of our world. As you follow on with me, try to recall when you have been stunned by some natural beauty: a sunset or sunrise or a rose in your own garden.

It's hard to describe such moments, isn't it? But let's give it a try. See if my attempt to get at such experiences matches your own experience.

At first, there's something like awe that such beauty exists and that I am in its presence. I also feel very happy, sometimes ready to shout for joy. I want to stay there and drink it in. It's as though I have hit the jackpot of beauty and want to keep it. If I have a camera with me, I take a picture to remind me of this vision and to show to friends. Almost always I feel a desire to share this with someone. Sr. Ligita must have had this same desire when she showed me her pictures. Sometimes I have almost immediately realized that I was in the presence of God's beauty and joy and thanked God; most of the time the realization of God's presence comes only after reflection on the experience.

Does this description, as poor as it is, come close to matching your own experience? If so, then we can say that we experience God's joy in the created beauties of this world. How would you describe your own experiences of recognizing God's presence in natural beauty? Maybe you want to tell God how happy God's joy makes you or just thank him.

Surprised by Joy

C. S. Lewis titled his memoir *Surprised by Joy*. The joy he refers to in the title is the desire for God. Early in life, he recounts, he had a couple of incidents where he was overcome with a sense of great well-being and a desire for he knew not what. He tells readers that he spent years searching for the satisfaction of this desire in all the wrong places until finally he realized that it was God he desired. He calls this desire joy because the desire itself gave him more happiness than any other pleasure he experienced.

What he describes, it seems to me, is what I am trying to express here. It's a feeling of great well-being accompanied by a deep wanting of something way beyond anything we have experienced. We don't have that "something," but the *desire* for it gives us great joy. Moreover, we want to keep that memory alive. Hence, we take pictures or write about it or want to tell someone else what we have seen or heard.

It was something like this joy that overcame me in a Houston, Texas, hotel room the day of Barack Obama's first inauguration. I was in Houston to give a talk that afternoon. In the morning I turned on the television. As I experienced the inauguration of the first African American president of the United States and saw the joy of the participants and felt my own joy, tears came to my eyes, the kind of tears I associate with experiences of the presence of God. Then to see Mr. and Mrs. Obama walking hand in hand down the street, broadly smiling, with cheering crowds all around was almost too much to bear alone. So I called a friend back in the Boston area to talk about it. It was a day of such hope for America and for the sense that, just possibly, our desire for the end of racism that has shadowed our country since its inception may finally be satisfied. I sensed that I was experiencing some of the joy of what God wants for our country and our world.

What desires have been joy for you? Can you identify an experience similar to mine in Houston, a time when you sensed that a deep desire might finally be fulfilled? Recall that memory as you talk with God.

A Little Boy

In September of 2018, we Jesuits celebrated the jubilees of our province with a Mass and dinner at Boston College High School. At the Mass I was sitting with some Jesuits in one row. In front of us were four adults with a small boy who was probably less than two years old. The adults were the grandparents and parents of the boy. Fairly soon after the parents entered the row, the grandfather took the boy from his mother and then held him in his arms for most of the Mass.

The first time he hoisted the boy so that the boy could see over his shoulder, I looked into his open, lovely face with bright eyes. When his eyes found mine, I spontaneously broke into a smile, and he smiled back in such a way that I felt great joy. Then he looked at one of the other Jesuits, and I saw the same open, lovely smile, and joy on the face of the Jesuit.

During that whole long Mass, the boy never uttered a whimper or gave any suggestion that he was anything but captivated by being there. At the same time, I noticed that the four adults had smiles on their faces as often as I noticed them and that they often looked with warmth and joy at the boy while also attending to what was happening at the altar.

At communion time the boy's mother took him back. After the Mass I tapped her on the shoulder and told her what a wonderful child she had. She said that they felt so lucky. I then said something like this: "I think that the clear love of parents and grandparents for the boy had something to do with his way of being." God was present not only in the Eucharist but also in that loving family.

Does this story remind you of anything in your own experience that, perhaps only in hindsight, you can see was the presence of our lovely God in ordinary life? Perhaps you will be more likely to notice God's presence as a result of reading these examples. Perhaps, too, you may want to talk to God about that experience now.

Another Story from the Mother of Three Little Boys

Do you remember the mother with the three sons of earlier chapters? Well, she told me another story that fits this chapter. The family was at the beach for a week's vacation. She was sitting on the beach reading while her husband and the boys fished for crabs off the pier. She heard their joyous whoops of laughter as they caught the crabs (and then threw them back into the water), counting the catch until they reached a new record, outdoing last year's record. As she listened, she felt the presence of God, who seemed to join her in her enjoyment of the joy of her family.

Have you ever experienced something like this, a joy that seemed to come out of nowhere, yet moved you deeply and perhaps made you grateful to be alive? Did you think of God at the time? Can you see now that it was a "God moment"? You can talk to God about that experience now, if you want to.

God's a Great Fan of Yours

A friend, Jim Menno, was golfing with two friends in Florida some years ago. The older friend said that he was on retreat once with a Jesuit priest. In a kind of wise-guy way he told the priest that he was a great fan of God. The priest responded with something that had puzzled him ever since: "God's a great fan of yours." That line went right to Jim's heart, and he said, "It's true, you know." He has never forgotten this event, and it gives him great joy whenever he thinks of it.

Here is another example of how someone, in this case Jim's friend, even without knowing it, was a sign of God's joy in us.

How does it feel to you to hear "God's a great fan of yours"? Perhaps you want to talk to God about your reactions.

Have you ever been stunned suddenly by something said about God and wondered about it, but never followed up to find out whether or not it was true? I hope that you will take seriously such wonder from now on and follow it up. When we wonder about something said about God, it's probably a sign that we should take it seriously and find out whether it's true or not. In Christian spirituality such a process is called discernment. In the last chapter you will find some ideas on the process of discernment, which I hope will be helpful.

Poetry and Music

Joy can hit us unexpectedly, as must have happened to Dante when he came to the end of his *Divine Comedy*. He has been led through hell, purgatory, and now heaven, quite a journey with great emotional ups and downs. But the end, it seems to me, is a quiet, joyful nod to the God who has been leading him all this way. These are the last lines of the whole poem:

> Here my powers rest from their high fantasy,
>   but already I could feel my being turned—
>
> . . . .
>
>   by the Love that moves the Sun and the
>   other stars.

That "Love that moves the sun and the other stars" has, of course, been drawing Dante's being all along. Perhaps only now, at the end of this great labor of love, does he realize the truth of what he writes. Perhaps he could realize what was drawing him all along this journey only when he was finished, could experience fully the joy of what he had created only with God's gracious help.

Something similar may have happened to Ludwig van Beethoven as he came to the end of his Ninth Symphony. The symphony touches on all the deepest emotions of the human heart, often enough lingering on the darker emotions. But at the end Beethoven was moved to write music to accompany the poet Schiller's *Ode to Joy*.

As the last movement gains steam, there seems to be a struggle between the darker emotions and some much brighter ones as the melody that will be used for the *Ode to Joy* tries to break through. Finally a male soloist calls out, *Nicht diese Töne*, "Not these tones," but these. Then he sings *Freude!* (Joy!), *Freude!* and follows with the first stanza of the ode. Other soloists and the full chorus take up the song of joy that celebrates the unity of humanity, God's dream for our world. Beethoven himself was completely deaf at this time of his life, but he still finished this last of his symphonies with the great musical *Ode to Joy*.

I'm strongly tempted to think of joy as another name for God when I hear the last movement of the Ninth Symphony. Like C. S. Lewis, I find myself often surprised by joy, and when tears come to my eyes, I am sure that the desire I feel is for God and that I am experiencing God's presence. How about you?

David Brooks: A Prophet for Our Times

As I was rewriting this chapter, David Brooks published one of his gems in the op-ed page of *The New York Times*, this one for Tuesday, May 7, 2019, titled "The Difference between Joy and Happiness." In it he contrasted the feelings of college graduates at their graduation, which Brooks named "happiness," from those of their parents, which he named "joy."

I'm not as sure as he is that these words have exactly the nuances he gives them, but I agree with the distinction he makes between what they might be feeling. The graduates themselves are happy because they have finished college; the grind is over. But Brooks says that the parents' feeling is not for themselves so much as for their children. This feeling is what Brooks calls joy.

His distinction fits this chapter, and I agree with his main point, namely, that rejoicing in another's good fortune is a deeper and more satisfying emotion than rejoicing in one's own good fortune. Brooks writes: "Happiness usually involves a victory for the self. Joy tends to involve the transcendence of self. Happiness comes from accomplishments. Joy comes when your heart is in another. . . . Joy is the present that life gives you as you give away your gifts." He continues:

> They say that love is blind, but the affection friends have for each other is the opposite of blind. It is ferociously attentive. You are vulnerable, and your friend holds your vulnerability. He pauses, and you wait for him. You err, and she forgives.

Brooks notes that we live in a time when vulnerability often leads to attacks rather than forgiveness, but he opts for vulnerability and friendship as antidotes for what ails our society. He ends his column with these words:

> Sometimes when you're out with your friends, you taste a kind of effervescent joy. . . . When you have moments like that you realize there is magic in the world. You can't create the magic intentionally, but when you are living at that deep affectionate level, it sometimes just combusts within you. A blaze of joy. (A23)

The kind of joy Brooks describes comes to us, I believe, when we act as images of God who must be joy itself. After all, God is love and must rejoice with us in all our joys and endeavors. When we rejoice with others, we are like God. Isn't that something to be grateful for?

God Delights in Beauty and Is Beauty

In *Speaking of Faith: Why Religion Matters—and How to Talk About It*, Krista Tippett tells of an interview with the Muslim thinker Khaled Abou El Fadl and a Jewish rabbi, Harold Schulweis. El Fadl "insists that the key to the future of Islam lies in recovering its 'core moral value of beauty': God delights in beauty, Islam teaches at its core, and is beauty. . . . Rabbi Schulweis responded in kind, recalling the evocative

Jewish biblical counterpart: 'the beauty of holiness.'"[12] In the discussion that followed, Tippett and these two men came

> to another kind of critique these religious men, a Jew and a Muslim, could make of actions done in the name of religion. Is it beautiful, or is it ugly? This question was proposed as a theological measuring stick, a credible litmus test. Does this action reveal a delight in this creation and in the image of a creative, merciful God who could have made it? Is it reverent with the mystery of that?[13]

These two men, in other words, were making the question of beauty the criterion for discernment of whether an action was of God or not. If an action that we intend does not, somehow, resonate with beauty, then we should be very wary of doing it. I like that. What do you think?

I encourage you to reflect on the beauty you have experienced—whether in nature or relationships or the arts. The loveliness around us can remind us of the generous creativity and infinite loveliness of God. Your conversation with God can consist of your simple thanks, wonder, and joy.

8

Lavish Generosity:
Our "Wow" Experiences

"In the beginning when God created the heavens and the earth . . ." (Genesis 1:1). The writer of Genesis is trying to describe what is impossible to describe. Before this "beginning" there is no time; indeed, there is nothing at all but God. Then everything we know begins: time and space and this vast universe. Everything that exists outside of God exists because God wants it. Talk about lavish generosity! If we can wrap our hearts and minds around this great mystery, then we know that *all* is gift. We would have to say that God is indeed lavishly generous, generous beyond measure. Gratitude is the most fundamental attitude and response of anyone who allows the reality of creation into his or her consciousness.

The "Wow" Experience

Think of all the various species of plants and animals that populate our planet: the variety and the beauty are staggering. We are surrounded by such riotous variety and beauty that we often are stunned and can just say, *Oh* or *Ah* or *Wow!* In her lovely book on the three essential prayers, *Help, Thanks, Wow*, Anne Lamott writes:

> The third great prayer, Wow, is often offered with a gasp, a sharp intake of breath, when we can't think of another way to capture the sight of shocking beauty or destruction, of a sudden unbidden insight or unexpected flash of grace. "Wow" means we are not dulled to wonder. We click into being fully present when we're stunned into that gasp, by the sight of a birth, or images of the World Trade Center towers falling, of the experience of being in a fjord, at dawn, for the first time. "Wow" is about having one's mind blown by the mesmerizing or the miraculous: the veins in a leaf, birdsong, volcanoes.[14]

She describes so well how we feel when we pay attention to what is all around us; we can really be staggered by the lavish generosity of our God, can't we?

A Suggestion for Contemplation

I suggest that you take some time to notice things around you. Look, listen, smell, taste, and touch what surrounds you. You'll be surprised by God, I'm sure. When we take time to smell the roses, as it were, we are focusing on something other than ourselves and our problems. Such smelling (or looking, tasting, etc.) can be a spiritual exercise: we forget ourselves, at least a little, and focus on the other. This can be called contemplation. What it does is quiet our inner lives so that God has a shot at surprising us.

As I write this section, in late October in New England, I can look out my windows, even on this wet and dreary Friday, and see breathtaking beauty as the trees, especially the maples, continue their slow decline toward a winter rest. Orange, red, pink, and yellow leaves abound. "Wow!" is the appropriate response. And *wow* can be a way of communicating to God how much we appreciate what God has done for us. Remember that the creator of all this seasonal beauty is God. It's as though God is saying to us, *How do you like that? And that? And that?* I can understand how the psalmist can exclaim, while contemplating the beauty of the temple in Jerusalem:

> One thing I asked of the LORD,
>   that will I seek after:

> to live in the house of the LORD
>   all the days of my life,
> to behold the beauty of the LORD,
>   and to inquire in his temple.

—Psalm 27:4

The Work of Artists

My friend Marika Geoghegan is an artist who puts together gorgeous colors that almost rival the colors of a New England fall. On occasion when I have seen some of her paintings, I have had the wow experience Anne Lamott writes about. I have in my room a framed collage she made of ripped colored papers. It is stunning in its simplicity and beauty and is a reminder of the great artistry of our creator God.

Perhaps you, too, have been knocked over by a beautiful landscape or abstract painting and know what I mean. If so, perhaps you, too, have been surprised by God as you admired the beauty created by another human being. Or the beauty you yourself have created. If you have not yet thought of such experiences as evidence of the presence of our surprising God, maybe from now on you will be more prone to notice the presence of the God of surprises.

Recall, too, what you read about my encounter with Sr. Ligita Ryliskyte's pictures of Bryce and Antelope Canyons. When I wrote that section, I did not know that this chapter was coming to me. The very writing of this book is, for me, a kind of wow experience. I am constantly being surprised by the lavish generosity of God.

"God Loves a Cheerful Giver"

In his second letter to the Corinthians, Paul writes, "God loves a cheerful giver" (2 Corinthians 9:7) while encouraging his readers to be generous. God is a cheerful giver; and since we are made in the image and likeness of God, we, too, are asked to be cheerful givers. I invite you now to think of times when you have been the recipient of lavish generosity by a cheerful giver.

Once when we were discussing generosity, a Jesuit told me about a pastor with whom he worked who gave, often through this Jesuit's hands, big gifts to some seminarians, who never thanked the pastor. My friend told me that he got angry at their apparent lack of gratitude and spoke to the pastor about this. The pastor sternly replied, "Am I to stop loving and giving simply because someone is incapable of expressing gratitude or returning love? The answer is an emphatic 'No'! That would be just too great a price to pay." My friend said it was a sober lesson learned and never forgotten. Here was a man who, like God, gave without counting the cost.

Maybe you have come across such lavish generosity. If so, then you have been in the presence of God whether you were aware of it or not. This reflection may increase the chances that the next time you meet such generosity you will be more attuned to the presence of God.

People Who Are Lavish in Their Hospitality and Generosity

I'm sure that, like me, you have met people who exude joy and are immensely attractive because of it. I mean people who just seem to be welcoming and glad to see you, even if you're a stranger to them.

If you come to their home, even unexpectedly, you are immediately welcomed and made to feel at home. Just now my parents came to mind. I recall how they always welcomed guests into our small flat and, if lunch or dinner were on, easily invited them to share the meal with us. I always felt comfortable bringing friends home, knowing that my mother and father would open their hearts and arms to them. This was true in high school as well as later when I became a Jesuit. Without knowing why, I always wanted my friends to meet my family. I now think the reason was that they were so open-hearted in welcoming others, the way God is.

I have dedicated this book to Mary and John Power. I had met Mary several times and then her husband, John. A few years ago, they invited me to dinner at their home. Margaret, one of their four children, was also present. It was an evening I will never forget. I was welcomed into their home and into their lives with open arms. We shared our joys and our struggles with an openness I have rarely felt so quickly established. We also laughed a great deal. I fell in love with this family that night and have since met the three other children. The children are like their parents, clearly at ease with one another and with other people. My friend Bill Russell, SJ, has been included in our get-togethers and agrees that it's a joy to be with this family.

Without much fanfare, Mary and John are very generous with their gifts and talents and their hospitality. They are, for me and, I'm sure, for many others, signs of God's lavish generosity. Perhaps you, too, have been gifted with such friends and know, through them, God's lavish generosity.

Mary and John Power are genuinely happy, joyful people. Of course, they have had their share of sorrow and pain, but that does not put much of a damper on their happiness and enjoyment of life.

I have come to believe that the happiest people I know are those who are generous toward others with their time, talent, and treasure. I feel very happy when I am able to help someone else. I have asked others how they feel when they help others in some way. Everyone agrees that helping others brings happiness. I have concluded that the reason for the happiness is that when we do something for someone else, especially someone in need, we are most like God, who is so lavishly generous to us.

Have you ever thought along these lines? If not, then perhaps you will begin to notice how happy you feel the next time you are helpful to someone else. When we are helpful to others, we are God's sacramental sign of his generous love. Once you are aware of such feelings, you have something else to talk over with God.

Asking Others for Help

Now I want to take the next step with you. If you are like me, you probably dislike asking for help. While I was writing this book, I had what turned out to be a nasty fall leading to a five-month stint in our nursing home. Being unable to take a shower by myself or to walk without help forced me to ask for help a lot. And it was freely and generously given by the staff of the nursing home and by fellow Jesuits and other friends. I realized that I was giving these people a chance to be images of God, and they came through big-time. Moreover, it seemed to me that they were happy to give me a hand. These months in the nursing home made it a lot easier for me to ask for help. I wish I had been humbler (and more trusting in others) earlier in life.

We all need one another in order to lead meaningful and happy lives; so why not count on the goodwill of others to be the images of our generous God they are created to be and ask for their help when needed? Doing so gives them a chance to act on their divine character as people made in God's image. It gives them the chance to experience the happiness that comes from being generous.

What do you think? Perhaps you want to talk with God about some of the people who have helped you or about how helping others has given you happiness. You could even ask God whether he enjoys giving to us. Perhaps our happiness in giving is just a faint echo of God's happiness in giving to us.

Two More Stories from the Mother with the Three Boys

The mother with the three boys has provided me with two more stories in which children become reflections of God's love. Remember that the oldest boy, whom I call Jason, was born with bilateral clubfeet. He needed regular therapy even after his two brothers were born. The first event occurred when their mother took all of them to Jason's therapy sessions. I call the two brothers David, age seven at the time of this story, and Michael, age five. Michael is the hero of the "beams of love" story. On this day, as their older brother did his various workouts, these two young boys shouted encouragement from the sidelines. "Way to go, Jason!" "You can do it, Jason!" "Yay, Jason, you're our hero!"

When the mother told me this story, I was moved at how these little boys were showing great love for their older and admired brother. I felt immediately that they were God's way of encouraging Jason in his difficult journey to full health of mind and body. They were signs of God's lavish love and presence for their mother and father as well, and for me when I heard the story, and, I hope, for you as you read it.

The next event occurred one evening as the mother was trying hard to get the three boys to bed at their usual time. The middle boy, David, always dawdles a bit. This night, everything was done for bed, but he said that he had something else he had to do. His mother told him that he was all set for bed, but he said, "I need to give Jason a hug." He got into bed with Jason, hugged him, and said, "I love you," and then went off to bed. David was again a sign of God's lavish love and comforting presence for Jason, for his mother, and, I hope, for all who read this story. Quite a family, isn't it?

Do these stories remind you of something similar? There are signs of God's love all around us, aren't there? Perhaps these stories have sparked a memory of having experienced something similar in your own family. Maybe you have something more to talk over with God.

An Elderly Runner

Let me finish this chapter with a remarkable story. The March 18, 2019, issue of *America* carried an article by Sr. Madonna Buder, who is now eighty-eight years old. At age forty-seven she started running and has since become a marathoner and a triathlete, even competing in Ironman triathlons, which require a 2.4-mile swim, a 112-mile bike ride, and a 26.2-mile run, all to be finished within 17 hours. At age eighty-two she became the oldest woman to finish an Ironman triathlon within the allotted time.

She writes: "While running out in God's nature, I would find a sense of calm and wellbeing. One day, it struck me that our problems are so minimal compared to the magnificence that surrounds us. The sport has taught me to be grateful for all that God gives us—even the injuries." Sr. Madonna has come to know of the lavish generosity of God through her life, but especially through her running.

Maybe you, too, have experienced God's lavish generosity through running or through some other sport or activity. Pause to consider where you have encountered God's lavish generosity—and feel free to voice your response in prayer.

9

God's Pleasure in Us

Have you ever thought that God might want to thank you or to congratulate you? Perhaps this is not a common feeling in most of us. We tend to focus on God's unhappiness with us, don't we? Yet there's reason to believe that God responds to our successes and good deeds as well as to our struggles and failures. God wants to build us up, not tear us down. In this chapter I want to encourage you to pay attention to times when you have felt encouragement or affirmation from someone, and ask yourself whether that person might have been God's way of responding to you and expressing God's pleasure at the good you have done.

An Unexpected Pick-Me-Up

Have you ever experienced a pick-me-up feeling from an unexpected source, such as being thanked out of the blue for doing something kind for someone else? This has happened to me a few times when I had not even thought that I was doing anything special.

One day the late Larry Corcoran, SJ, took me aside to tell me that I had been very compassionate to some Jesuits in our community, and he mentioned their names. I was rather stunned. First of all, males don't often take the time to speak this way to one another. Moreover, I had spent some time with these men but had not considered it a duty. I just did it. At any rate, I felt that God was telling me through Larry that he was pleased with me, and I was very grateful.

In November of 2018, I was proved wrong again about males. I ran into Kevin White, a Jesuit friend who had just spent a few years working in Africa with the Jesuit Refugee Service (JRS). He was staying with us at Campion Center for a couple of months until he joined the Jesuit Refugee Service office in Geneva for his next assignment. He said that during the previous year I had said something that touched him deeply and had a very positive effect on his ministry in Africa. He had given a talk to our community about the work of JRS in Africa. Another Jesuit had asked him what he would do for people whose misery seemed unsolvable, and he had been a bit flustered by the question. Afterward I stopped him and said, "What all of us can at least give to people, no matter how desperate their circumstances, is our presence and our compassion." This comment, he said, had burnt into his heart and helped him in his work with JRS. In addition, it fit into the motto of what JRS tries to do for refugees: accompaniment. I was deeply moved by his comment to me and told him how grateful I was.

Later in the day, as I reflected on this encounter, I thanked God for what Kevin had said and told God that I took Kevin's comment to me as being God's way of speaking to me. In addition, I realized how my words to Kevin helped him to be God's presence in his difficult mission. God was telling me, through Kevin, that God appreciates what I say about him. Actually, what I said to Kevin came from my own experience of feeling compassion for God, who very often can only be present to people who are suffering without being able to change the circumstances of their lives.

How do you react to this story? Does it remind you of something in your own life? Perhaps you have been God's sacramental sign for others by thanking them for something they did or said. I hope that these stories will help you notice how often God is present to you through other people and lead you to deeper conversations with God.

Looking at Others as Persons

As if to assure me of what I just wrote about God being present to people, I had the following experience around the same time. I was directing the retreat of Tom Bradshaw, a lawyer from Kansas City, Missouri. Tom had organized a group of lawyers to do pro bono work for poor people. When he read of Pope Francis saying that Christians should look at those they are helping, he realized that he had been treating poor clients as "cases" rather than as persons.

Soon after that, a man was referred to him who had a few misdemeanors on his record but was trying to move ahead with his life in a new direction. This record would make it hard for him to work in his new field. He wanted to know if the record could be cleared. After talking with him about his legal needs, Tom asked him a bit about his life, and they had a fine conversation. As the man was getting ready to leave, he said, "This is the first time anyone has listened to me." Needless to say, this touched Tom deeply. His telling me touched me, too. Tom had acted as an image of God for this man. With his comment the man had affirmed Tom and thus became God's way of thanking Tom for following Pope Francis's suggestion.

The same Tom was speaking with Anne Copponi, the administrative assistant to the director of Campion Renewal

Center. He thanked her for the retreat director he had. She said something about how much he was loved and pointed upward. He knew immediately that she meant God and as immediately felt that she had given him a glimpse of the God he was seeking in the retreat. Here Anne helped Tom to have a sense of how God led him to this retreat and to me. I, of course, was deeply moved when Tom told me of this encounter and felt God's affirmation of my way of directing retreats.

God is constantly revealing Godself in our various relationships, as we notice one another and either receive help or offer help. But notice how God's love and character come full circle when we all talk with one another. One person thanks another for what he or she did that was helpful. Someone passes along to you the gratitude or compliment, yet another person has mentioned about you—information you would not otherwise have had. One person responds with gratitude to another's gift; another person recognizes in someone a gift that that person did not even see as anything special or helpful. All of us reflect God to one another as we notice what is happening around us—and then speak up about it. Here again we see how love can be contagious.

God's Affirmation Experienced Almost Accidentally

One afternoon a woman told me in a session of spiritual direction how she experienced God's presence at Eastern Point Retreat House in Gloucester, Massachusetts. Her parish was having a weekend retreat there in November, the month when we remember our beloved dead. She had been asked to lead the group in an exercise of remembrance of people they had lost through death or divorce or any other way. After she made her presentation, she suggested that each one turn to a neighbor and have a chat about the losses they had remembered.

The leader herself did not have a partner. So she just listened in silence to the sounds of the ocean. As she listened, she began to hear snippets of the various conversations, sometimes the name of a person, sometimes an expression of sadness or joy at the memory of someone. She felt that she was surrounded by God, although the full impact of the experience hit her only sometime later. God seemed to be grateful for what she had done with the group. Again, she met God through others, who themselves were meeting God through interaction.

Has anything like this happened to you? If so, did you think of God acting at that time? Maybe the stories you read here will encourage you to become more attentive to God's interventions in your own life.

A Chain Reaction

I'm often surprised and very pleased to hear from readers I don't know telling me how my books have helped them in their relationship with God. This is music to my ears because I write to help people come closer to God. In the past year, one letter especially delighted me. And I took it as God's way of showing his appreciation of what I had written and done.

A woman sent me a letter telling me how much she was helped by my book *Praying the Truth*. She went on to say that she had given it to her granddaughter, who was in jail awaiting trial on some charge. The letter contained a card that her granddaughter made for her in jail. Let's call the granddaughter Leah. The grandmother wrote me that "in the midst of a situation that must be painful and lonely, this forced confinement is obviously providing fertile ground. The post card speaks clearly of that." The card is homemade with a picture cut out of a farm magazine. Leah writes:

> I used toothpaste in lieu of glue. So I hope it holds (I'm sure that it will smell minty fresh!). I've been so into *Praying the Truth* the last few days. I never realized before

how much I was keeping from my prayers, and how good it is to let God into all aspects of my life and being. So cool, so important. I love you.

Two people communicated to me God's pleasure at my work through that book. Leah, of course, but also her grandmother, who took the time to write to me and include Leah's lovely card. Thank you, Leah! Thank you, Grandma! Thank you, God!

This story continues. After I finished the last paragraph, I sent it to the grandmother, asking her to see if Leah was okay with my using it in this book. She wrote this back to me just after Leah had surprisingly received a tough sentence.

> Thank you for your note and the words you wrote about Leah that may be included in the book. Leah's Mom (my daughter) was here for the weekend, and during a phone call to Leah she read her your thoughts. Leah was literally moved to tears. Happy ones. The timing of this could not have been better. It certainly was a source of comfort, affirmation, really, for her.

In addition, the grandmother included a short excerpt from her daughter that indicated that Leah and her mother were greatly comforted by reading together a portion of a chapter of *Praying the Truth*.

Notice in this story how one good deed leads to another and another. It's like a contagion, isn't it, again a contagion of goodness. Does this story remind you of anything that has happened in your own life? Have you noticed a contagion of kind gestures breaking out someplace? This is the kind of contagion our world desperately needs.

Let me finish this story of Leah. As I said before, early in 2019 I spent five months in the nursing facility at Campion Center. Just as I began my stint in the nursing home, I received a letter from Leah, who is now in prison. It was a gift of God to me as I began this difficult time of my life. In it she wrote:

> You absolutely delighted us with your response and we're so thrilled that you'd like to include a bit about us in your upcoming book. I was beaming for days after receiving a copy of your latest letter. Really it's been such a blessing to me and my whole family to be in touch with you and to feel recognized like that.
>
> As my relationship with God has deepened, I've been able to connect more deeply with every human in my life. For the longest time there was something getting in between me and the love of God and me and the love of others, and that barrier is untruth; in the form of lies or of unspokenness; untruth divides us from God and from our loved ones and from the world. . . .

Point being, your book (*Praying the Truth*) reflects the preciousness of truth in all relationships, and it opened me up. First to God, and then, as I'm finding is often the natural following effect of a step forward spiritually, with everyone and everything around me. . . . You are truly a conduit for God's truth and a blessing for me and for (my) clan.

Leah expresses in her own way my conviction that getting close to God opens us up to openness to others and, indeed, to the whole world. Needless to say, Leah's letter picked up my spirits at a dark time in my life. She was a sign of God's care for me when I needed it badly and also, I thought, she was a sign of God's gratitude.

The Effects of Honest Sharing

We never know how something true that we say may affect another or others. Have you ever had the experience of having someone tell you that something you said or did had had a great effect on his or her life? Sometimes I can't even remember what I said, but whatever it was, even if I was misinterpreted, it had a good effect on someone else. I have taken these events as an indication that God has used me as a sign of his presence. (I've also had people tell me that remarks I made hurt them or angered them. Sometimes I have remembered speaking out of turn, sometimes I have not remembered. I mention this, just to speak the whole truth.) Perhaps you have had similar experiences. Have you ever thought that God used you as a way to say something to another? For us believers it's very possible. Remarkable, isn't it? Maybe you have something new to talk over with God.

My friend Marika Geoghegan, the artist, had such an experience recently. She was a frequent attendee at a meeting in her city at one time, but about ten years elapsed before she recently returned to that meeting. After the meeting a woman came over to her and said how happy she was to see her again and then went on to tell Marika that a remark she made years ago had changed her life.

At the earlier meeting Marika had said that she did her artwork at the table in her house. This intrigued the woman who had always felt she wanted to do artwork but was blocked by feeling that she needed more space, perhaps even a studio.

At any rate, she started painting after that meeting and now had a new lease on life. She had a house full of her work and invited Marika to come over to see it. Marika was bowled over by the beauty this woman was creating. Since that time, they have become friends. Marika experienced God's gratitude for her generosity in sharing her experience through this encounter ten years or so later.

A seemingly chance remark changed this woman's life for the better. But her telling Marika of the effect of her words also affected Marika. She felt affirmed. I see the hand of God in this event, don't you? We never know how speaking honestly about ourselves affects others for the better. God inspires us even when we are not aware of it and also inspires others to hear what they need to hear at a particular time. And then inspires the hearers to thank the one who spoke, thus continuing the contagion of goodness.

A High School Rendition of *Les Misérables*

Mary Fitzgerald, a friend, told me a story that was deeply moving both for her and for me as I heard it. She had invited five of her closest friends to attend a performance by Canton High School students of *Les Mis*. Mary's granddaughter had a starring role. This is how Mary described what happened.

> Before the play started, I was standing at the end of our row and looked at the faces of my five friends. I said a quick prayer of gratitude that I had them in my life. I then was overwhelmed by the sense of goodness. My heart leaped up; every fiber of my body felt goodness. Rosemary, my friend of forty-five years, said, almost at the same time, "I'm so glad that you invited me. I feel such goodness."

The play started; with every song, every theme, you sensed goodness from these youngsters. Their faces shone with goodness. There was a darling freshman with Down syndrome whom the other youngsters nurtured and loved through all the practices and took out to cast parties. She made a few mistakes in her role, but one girl just took her hand and helped her without much ado about it. The girl herself shone with joy through her steps.

The perfect ending for this proud Grammy was Kayla, who played Cosette and sang "A Heart Full of Love." I witnessed that love in the cast, in my friends, in the parents, in the messages of the play enacted by a beautiful group of high schoolers.

I've never witnessed so many beautiful tears in all of us who were there that evening. The whole evening was, for me, filled with the presence of God's love.

My friends all had the same experience of goodness, love, teamwork, joy, and talent.

Here is an example of how God shows appreciation for people through others, in this case through Mary Fitzgerald's willingness to publish her reactions to the musical. Mary felt that the audience was caught up in God's joy, goodness, and love through the way these high school actors performed *Les Misérables*. She felt God's gratitude for what happened that evening.

Have you ever had any experiences like Mary's? Did you think you were in God's presence on those occasions? If not, perhaps you will be more aware of the surprising presence of God in your ordinary life. God is surprising us all the time, isn't he? It's rather amazing how present God is in what seem to be totally secular events.

10

God Comforts the Afflicted

Although in Catholic piety "Comforter of the Afflicted" is most often associated with Mary the mother of Jesus, in Scripture the original comforter of the afflicted is God.

Some Biblical Examples

For example, in Psalm 27 we read:

> The LORD is my light and my salvation;
>   whom shall I fear?
> The LORD is the stronghold of my life;
>   of whom shall I be afraid?
> When evildoers assail me
>   to devour my flesh—
> my adversaries and foes—
>   they shall stumble and fall.
> Though an army encamp against me,
>   my heart shall not fear;

though war rise up against me,
   yet I will be confident.
One thing I asked of the LORD,
   that will I seek after:
to live in the house of the LORD
   all the days of my life,
to behold the beauty of the LORD,
   and to inquire in his temple.
For he will hide me in his shelter
   in the day of trouble;
he will conceal me under the cover of his tent;
   he will set me high on a rock.

—Psalm 27:1–5

Not only does God comfort this afflicted man, but he also saves him from his enemies. Notice, too, that the psalmist delights in the "beauty of the LORD" and wants "to live in the house of the LORD" all the days of his life.

The same theme comes through in Psalm 42:

As a deer longs for flowing streams,
   so my soul longs for you, O God.
My soul thirsts for God,
   for the living God.
When shall I come and behold
   the face of God?
My tears have been my food
   day and night,

while people say to me continually,
    "Where is your God?"
These things I remember,
    as I pour out my soul:
how I went with the throng,
    and led them in procession to the house of God,
with glad shouts and songs of thanksgiving,
    a multitude keeping festival.
Why are you cast down, O my soul,
    and why are you disquieted within me?
Hope in God; for I shall again praise him,
    my help and my God.
My soul is cast down within me;
    therefore I remember you
from the land of Jordan and of Hermon,
    from Mount Mizar.

—Psalm 42:1–6

When God gives his teachings to the Israelites in the desert, he reminds them to care for the poor, the alien, and the afflicted, as he does. Here are two verses in Leviticus from a listing of God's commandments:

When you reap the harvest of your land, you shall not reap to the very edges of your field, or gather the gleanings of your harvest. You shall not strip your vineyard bare, or gather the fallen grapes of your vineyard; you shall leave them for the poor and the alien: I am the LORD your God. (Leviticus 19:9–10)

God has a soft spot in his heart for those who are afflicted by life's difficulties. And he wants to make sure that his chosen people have the same softness of heart. By the way, he means us, too.

Jesus knew of God's predilection for the afflicted. In the Sermon on the Mount he said, "Blessed are those who mourn, for they will be comforted" (Matthew 5:4). The apostle Paul knew of this predilection as well and showed it when he wrote:

Blessed be the God and Father of our Lord Jesus Christ, the Father of mercies and the God of all consolation, who consoles us in all our affliction, so that we may be able to console those who are in any affliction with the consolation with which we ourselves are consoled by God. For just as the sufferings of Christ are abundant for us, so also our consolation is abundant through Christ. If we are being afflicted, it is for your consolation and salvation; if we are being consoled, it is for your consolation, which you experience when you patiently endure the same sufferings that we are also suffering. (2 Corinthians 1:3–6)

So, let's take it that God is the comforter of the afflicted. Do we experience that comfort when we feel afflicted?

My Own Experience as an Elderly Jesuit

In this chapter I want to look at how God comforts the afflicted, which includes most of the Jesuits living here at Campion Center. Our Jesuit community has a two-pronged mission: to pray for the church and the Society of Jesus as we move ever more deeply into our last years of life and to offer hospitality and spiritual counsel and retreats to those who come to our large house.

Most of the Jesuits live in the Health and Wellness center. But even those of us who are not yet assigned to that center are past the prime of our lives. Our average age is over eighty. Most of us are experiencing the losses and the joys that come with aging and approaching death. We are among the afflicted, you might say.

But if you came to visit our community, you would find a lot of joy and humor mixed in with the suffering. I have to say that this community, in which I have lived for twenty-two years, is the best large Jesuit community I've ever lived in. I say that not just to make us look good but because it is actually quite astonishing to realize how much happiness and joy the community exudes.

Mind you, we are well aware of our flaws and foibles, our failures to be images of God, and our sins. I don't think any of us in his right mind would think that we deserve credit for the kind of real happiness we enjoy, for the most part. We don't think, for example, that God is lucky to have us on his side! We feel lucky to be Jesuits and to have such a generally happy community life. Nonetheless, I believe that we are, for one another, signs of how God wants to comfort us as we face aging and death.

Another of the reasons we feel so good, I'm sure, is the care and kindness of the staff of Campion Center. Many of the people who work here have been employees for years, some of them approaching thirty years. They know our names, and most of us know theirs. Our interactions in the dining room and hallways are often characterized by humorous banter, but always by kindness and care.

During my recent recuperation I was sometimes reduced to tears of gratitude by the care I received from the nurses, doctors, nursing assistants, and other staff of the house. We have won the lottery of love, to quote a phrase coined by Darrell Jones after he was released from prison and spent some months living with us. I feel that we Jesuits have won the lottery of love here at Campion. The members of our staff have been images of God, comforting us who are feeling the effects of aging and illness. Our staff are comforters of the afflicted for us and thus signs of God's comfort.

What comfort have you experienced when you were afflicted in some way? At the time, did you think of certain people as becoming God's surrogates, acting on God's behalf to give you comfort? If you didn't, perhaps you will begin to notice the surprising presence of God in the future. As you ponder these questions, you may realize that you have something to talk over with God.

A Funeral Homily Shows God's Desire to Comfort the Afflicted

Needless to say, a community like ours experiences a lot of death. You might think that these experiences would lead to a sense of impending doom, but that is not the case. Partly, I'm sure, the upbeat nature of our community has to do with the fact that we are a praying group.

For example, some years ago, a man who had had to undergo kidney dialysis for years was faced with the failure of the kinds of dialysis he had undergone. The doctors told him of his choices. He responded, "The one choice you didn't mention is that I stop treatment altogether and go home to God, something I have wanted all my life." This man had for years performed his own dialysis while continuing his work teaching at a university and then had gone to the hospital for a new kind of dialysis when the one he was doing himself no longer worked. Now that that form of dialysis had also failed, he was not morbid or depressed.

He just expressed what many of us hope to be able to do, to say that enough is enough, and move into the mystery of death with trust that "all shall be well, and all manner of thing shall be well" (Julian of Norwich), even beyond the grave.

We do experience God as comforter in our sorrow at the loss of a brother. For one thing, we have seen most of them grow progressively weaker so that death comes as a relief for the man himself. In addition, very often we are made aware that someone is close to death so that we can pray for him and say goodbye to him. Finally, the wake and funeral liturgy with its homily give us a chance to reflect on the life of our brother. We end each funeral liturgy just before the body is taken to the cemetery by singing in Latin the beautiful Gregorian chant *Salve Regina*.

One recent funeral homily stood out for me because it spoke not only to our feeling of loss but also to our present situation at Campion. The funeral liturgy was for James Keegan, SJ, a well-known spiritual director who was stricken with Parkinson's disease at least ten years before he died. Jim wrote poems about his struggles with the disease, expressing his anger and frustration, but also his humor and acceptance. The homily was delivered by Richard Boll-man, SJ, a dear friend of Jim's for about thirty-five years. It was a friendship that lasted even though most often they lived in different parts of the country. I think that parts of the homily will be a sign of God's presence for you the reader as the whole homily was for those of us present at the liturgy.

> I want to look back through this Gospel I just read [John 21:15–19]. It suggests that a follower of Jesus might well expect his later years could involve some limitations in freedom, unwanted turns in the road, being led by another where you don't want to go. . . . "Being led by another where you don't want to go. It's not because you've done something wrong. It's not the result of failure or weariness. I think something more blessed and hopeful goes on in a person's life, through illness, through limits. Maybe it can be called a new stage of formation. . . . Like the more we know our-selves in our limitations, the more we come to know Jesus as he is, who asks of us total trust in a new way: even in a broken body or the frustration of not being able to keep up a conversation, or to care for yourself going to bed and getting up in the mornings. A new time of formation.
>
> . . . I kept wanting to pretend Jim was better off than he really was. I think that was a mistaken effort on my

part. When I just allowed for his limits, I think we got closer to an enjoyment of one another. He was able to teach me how to value life differently. . . . So, as you also found, you who have lived with Jim and visited, it is no disgrace to be led by another to a place you can't get to alone. It is a pathway closer to Jesus.

. . . To have something to do in visiting him this last time . . . I reached for his book of poems. And there it all was, what he had to say to me about suffering, being led, the "margins of hell," the revolt of his body, the shame and his own anger too. The poems do not shut you out but draw you closer in, toward the mystery of letting Christ come close. And there Jim was all along. As if in the writing of the poems, in that private demanding work he had put aside childish ways of pleasing a person by reminiscing, and was simply here, being known for himself.

Jim learned to let himself be drawn to what God was giving him. It is born from the broken places, from seeds that die. And now it rises up real and sustained, and permanent, as we dare to think. Maybe as we remember our brother and friend, we can come to feel drawn to where Christ leads each of us. It is the heart of being formed, led even where we don't want to go, letting Christ have us entirely.

Rich Bollman was the voice of God for us who were present at Jim Keegan's funeral liturgy. It was a comfort not only for our loss of Jim and for all the losses we had seen him experience during his years at Campion but also for our own losses as we are led by another on a way we have not chosen.

The homily reminded me of the times when I felt the comforting presence of God while talking with Jim about his own sense of God's presence that allowed him to speak, often with humor, about his struggles with Parkinson's. I hope that it also speaks of God's desire to comfort you in your times of affliction.

One of the editors of this book was moved to tears in reading Rich Bollman's homily and then spoke to God about her reactions. Perhaps your reflections on this homily and on your own experiences of loss will lead you to have a conversation with God. That would be a happy result of reading parts of this homily.

Wisdom from Paul Crowley, SJ

Paul Crowley, SJ, a theology professor at Santa Clara University, is undergoing an aggressive treatment for cancer as I write. He sends out blogs occasionally. On November 28, 2018, he included a brief homily he delivered that day. Again, I believe his words remind us that God is comforter of the afflicted in difficult times. Here is the gist of what he wrote:

In these days leading up to Advent, we continue to be treated to explosive imagery, now in the Gospels themselves. Each of the Synoptic Gospels has a "little apocalypse," giving us a sense of the outlook of people in the wake of the Roman siege of Jerusalem and the destruction of the Temple in 70 A.D. These little apocalypses disclose the panic and fear that people were feeling at the time—perhaps not unlike the fear people today feel in the wake of mass shootings, megafires, hurricanes, climate change, ecological devastation, the resurgence of anti-Semitism and racism, the worldwide surging of refugees seeking safe haven from violence and death, the implosion of institutions, and the moral instability of our elected leaders. And each of us has our "little apocalypses"—life-changing tragedies, losses, or impossibilities with which we must somehow cope. In the Gospel today, the memory of Jesus is set within the context of such a wide amphitheater of suffering and fear. Yet he counsels: Do not be terrified; do not be afraid. I am here; God remains present in the midst of all of this.

What this means is that we have good reason to enter the present historical moment in a spirit of courage, even hope. And we can face our own "apocalypses" with courage, too. Yes we must always work against the forces of evil and falsehood in our midst; Jesus warns against false leaders who would manipulate fear with their lies (and of this we have ample evidence; there are Herods in every generation). But, Jesus points out, the real sense of crisis we experience does not point to the end of the world in a literal sense—only to the end of the world as we know it. For, in the eyes of a hope-filled faith, these crisis points, these signs, are oblique harbingers of a "new heaven and a new earth" (Revelation 21) that God is already bringing about, even though we cannot always see this happening because of our creaturely myopia and fear of change. Yet we have the assurance that nothing whatsoever, no form of suffering and not even death itself, can stand between us and the love of God in Jesus Christ (Romans 8). Love is the one thing that remains and upon which we can build a future.

In times of fear, then, and even in the face of death, we are not alone. We can move forward in courage on a road paved by hope.

In our time of trial and affliction Paul Crowley speaks God's word to me and, I hope, to you. He calls forth our faith in our God, who promises us that in spite of how things may look, "all shall be well, and all manner of thing shall be well" (the words Julian of Norwich heard in her vision when she and everyone around her thought she was dying and while Europe was ravaged by the Black Plague). Believers in God live with this conviction. "I believe, help my unbelief," I often pray, because at times I fear for the future of our world. If you are so moved, you might want to talk with God about your own reactions to the trials of our present age.

One final story may remind you of some experiences you have had or have heard of where God comforted the afflicted in awful circumstances. A woman and her husband were driving back home from a short vacation when their car was hit head-on by another car, which was speeding in the opposite direction, lost control, and crossed the double yellow line at a speed of 120 miles per hour. The wife wrote to me to tell me how her husband died. She was badly injured in the crash, but he died.

> For me, it has been a good year, a painful year, one of powerlessness, despair, of awe and wonder at the mystery called life. At the accident, my husband, slumped in the seat beside me, scanned me up and down with his still twinkling blue eyes, drew a final breath and said, "I love you." What an amazing gift that was for me. I don't think if I hadn't begun the contemplative journey myself, I would have seen it as such. Life seems to be Life, giving what it does. Through all the losses of this year, I get to choose to say thank you for all and for the blessings that God hides in everything.

Her husband, at that last moment of his life, as, no doubt often during his life, was able to be the sign of God's great love for his wife; comforter of the afflicted, indeed.

When have you felt God's comforting presence through another or were yourself, by the grace of God, such a comforting presence for somebody else? Don't we have much for which to be grateful?

11

God Afflicts the Comfortable

The Israelites often found God rather uncomfortable to be near. The Bible frequently depicts God as quite angry at their infidelities. I offer only one example, but one that almost led to the total destruction of the Israelites. While Moses was on the mountain with God, receiving the Ten Commandments, the Israelites persuaded Aaron to make a golden calf for them to worship. God blew up, as it were: "The Lord said to Moses, 'I have seen this people, how stiff-necked they are. Now let me alone, so that my wrath may burn hot against them and I may consume them; and of you I will make a great nation'" (Exodus 32:9–10). Moses stepped in to calm God down and thus saved the Israelites, but only barely, it seems. In the Gospels, Jesus often enough makes us uncomfortable with his demands and his anger. I remember that a Dutch Jesuit once called Jesus a difficult friend.

The Holy Spirit as Coach

In his Pentecost homily of 2019, Walter Smith, SJ, superior of my community, used the analogy of a coach for the Holy Spirit. He spoke of what a coach or manager does for his players, and mentioned that Tom Landry, legendary coach of the Dallas Cowboys of the National Football League, once said something along these lines, "A coach gets the players to do what they do not want to do in order to reach something they really want." Fr. Smith then went on to liken the role of the Holy Spirit to such a coach; the Holy Spirit tries to get us to do what we do not want to do so that we can achieve what we really want.

The question is, Do we meet the Holy Spirit as a difficult friend in our own lives? I believe that we do. The following examples may jog your own memories of being made uncomfortable by someone or something.

Family, Friends, and Others as God's Voice

I have had friends who told me difficult things. One time, when I was Provincial of the New England Jesuits, I got into a funk about something that happened in our community. I didn't know that it was obvious, but my friend Bill Russell, a member of the provincial staff, noticed. He told me in a caring way that my funk was having a negative effect on the community. As a result, I changed my attitude and apologized at the next community meeting. I believe that Bill acted as God's stand-in in that instance. I also remember that Fr. Paul Lucey, SJ, my spiritual director and confessor many years ago, told me, "You always say the same things in confession." At that time confessions were a weekly affair. Again, that was a wake-up call. Confession was, for me, often a rote exercise where I just repeated the same old sins every week. After that, I began to wonder whether weekly confession was a good idea and also began to take confession more seriously. Perhaps you are reminded of such an intervention in your own life.

Sometimes homilists can be uncomfortable friends. You may have experienced becoming uncomfortable during a homily. Some theology books have been God's uncomfortable friends for me, alerting me that I'd developed a way of thinking and acting that was not in tune with God's dream for our world. I hope that something like this has happened to you. If it hasn't, then perhaps you have not been hearing God's word preached or explained in writing.

If you are reminded of some time when a homily or a book shook your comfort level in a good way, you can thank God for the nudge and engage him in a conversation about it.

Parents often must question the behavior of their children or discipline them. Many of you know this from experience.

Have you ever seen yourself as God's agent when you have tried to help your children to be better young people? If these questions have reminded you of earlier experiences, you may want to have a conversation with God about them.

Speaking the Truth in Love

Often enough we don't know how to speak the truth in love to someone who needs to be told the truth. I confess to being in this position. But I have learned through hard experience that silence often is the worst way to deal with the problematic behavior of someone in the family or community.

For example, we see a family member, a friend, a close associate drinking alcohol and often getting drunk, and we don't know what to do or whether we should do anything. As a result, things often go from bad to worse. Yet Alcoholics Anonymous has been able to help millions throughout the world. And any recovering alcoholic will tell you how much they appreciate those who confronted them in love about their drinking. Of course, that was very often not their first reaction; they might have been very angry and defensive when confronted, but if they have finally acted on the intervention to get help, usually through a Twelve Step program, they are very grateful to those who intervened on their behalf. For them, those who intervened were the stand-ins for God. This kind of intervention is an instance where the Holy Spirit is like a coach, isn't it?

I am one of those alcoholics and am very grateful to those who tried to intervene earlier, and finally to a dear friend who confronted me in tears. They were all uncomfortable friends, God's stand-ins.

What do you think? Have you ever been confronted in love by friends or family members about your behavior and been changed as a result? Perhaps you have been an uncomfortable friend for someone. Perhaps you did not think of yourself as God's stand-in at the time, but now you can look back on that time and see that God was moving you to this act of love. The Spirit of God is always trying to draw us to live with more integrity as God's images. You may be led now to a conversation with God about your remembrances.

Spiritual Directors

Just as Paul Lucey, SJ, my earlier spiritual director, confronted me, so, too, in my long practice as a spiritual director for others, I have had to confront them by speaking the truth in love. It took me some time to become relatively comfortable with doing it, but I realized that it was the only way to be true to what the other person has asked of me, namely, to help them grow in their relationship with God. What I have found is that when I do bring up the uncomfortable truth with the other, I feel more whole and more in tune with God. At times the other is flummoxed and even angered by the truth, but in my experience, over time, if the person keeps praying, he or she begins to see the truth and finds that it sets them free.

Being Discomfited by Political Events

As I have been writing this book, I have become aware of how often I am made uncomfortable by what is going on in our country and in our church. In both civil and church life, anger and fierce condemnations seem to rule the day. In our country, it seems, you are either for or against President Trump, and those who disagree with you are the enemy, sometimes even the tools of Satan. In the church, the same dynamic seems to be happening with regard to attitudes toward Pope Francis and to controversial moral issues.

I believe that my discomfort was a sign from God that I needed to change my own attitudes both with regard to our presidential politics and the conflicts in the church. I

am not an unbiased participant here. I have strong leanings
in one direction in both cases, and though I try not to show
it, I have a tendency to denigrate the opinions of those on
the other side of the arguments. In other words, I have been
part of the problem, not of the solution.

Columnist David Brooks confirmed this in his column
in *The New York Times* op-ed page for March 18, 2019.
First he asks, "How do you answer hatred? How do you
respond when your political opponents assault you with
insult, stereotype and contempt? That's the moral question
we all have to answer during this election campaign."

He then points out that there are at least two possible
responses. You can respond in kind, meeting vitriol with vitriol, or you can refuse to respond in kind and still consider
your opponents as fellow citizens who have a different opinion. Brooks notes that most politicians in both parties are in
the first camp, fighting fire with fire, which only leads to a
bigger fire.

He goes on to extol one of the candidates who at least at
the beginning of his campaign wants to engage in a civilized
campaign and believes that the character of the candidate
is as important as his program. Brooks writes that "fanaticism is not the normal human state. Fanaticism is a disease
that grows out of existential anxiety. . . . The disease is in

our context and not in our souls. And that context can be changed with better leadership."[15]

Whether David Brooks knows it or not, he is acting as an image of God who does afflict the comfortable with the truth. Many of his columns return to the theme of this one and call us to be better persons. I think he is one of God's stand-ins for us Americans.

Perhaps you, too, have been made uncomfortable in a good way by the comments of someone you have read. Then perhaps you, too, can say that you have met God as a difficult, but really good friend, and you may want to engage in a conversation with God about your reactions.

Love the Planet

More and more of us have become aware, in recent years, of how devastating for the future of our planet human actions have become. There is now a scientific consensus that global warming has become a clear and present danger to future flourishing on planet Earth and that this warming has been exacerbated, if not primarily caused, by human actions. Thomas Berry, CP, was one of the early discomforters of the comfortable on the dangers we faced. His was, unfortunately, like a voice crying in the wilderness that not too many heard. One of my present companions,

John Surrette, SJ, however, did hear him and did his best to make the message heard, again without making much of an impact among large numbers of Catholics. However, with his encyclical *Laudato si'*, Pope Francis has taken up the banner for the salvation of our planet in the name of the Roman Catholic Church. Unfortunately, we still need more discomfiting so that a large enough number of us can make a real difference politically.

As I was rewriting this chapter, in the third week of Lent, 2019, I came upon the following Lenten reflection, one of the daily such reflections organized by the Ignatian Solidarity Network for Lent of 2019. It's by Brenna Davis, for Friday, March 29, 2019. It's titled "Our Greatest Commandment" because it's a comment on the Gospel reading of the day, on the two great commandments. It struck me as another instance of someone being God's discomforter of the comfortable and a gift of God for this book. Perhaps it will touch you, as well as be a gentle reminder of the kindness and mercy of God and of our creation as images of God.

> As someone who is especially passionate about environmental justice and climate change and how these issues affect the lives of the people who are most vulnerable, it is easy to be overwhelmed by the immense pressure

of the time in which we live. The weight and complexity of this reality can easily leave us feeling paralyzed and tempted to ignore climate change in this moment when we need to take prophetic action.

It's ironic that a focus on sustainability can leave us feeling so withered; however, in today's gospel, Jesus invites us to turn toward love that will *sustain us* in our work for climate justice.

"Love your God with all your heart, soul, mind, and strength and love your neighbor as you love yourself."

Our greatest commandment is not to single-handedly fix the climate or to completely eliminate carbon emissions but rather to love God and the people around us—to *care* for creation. A shift in focus to love and encounter will draw us into hopeful and creative ways of moving forward instead of being frozen by fear, our greatest temptation.

We find ourselves in the middle of Lent and in the midst of a climate crisis. Easter feels far away, and we don't know how everything is going to turn out; however, Thomas Merton reminds us that "Christian hope begins where every other hope stands frozen stiff before the face of The Unspeakable." Our work, like Jesus', begins where and when things seem most hopeless. This Lent we are called to follow in the footsteps of Jesus, not to remain paralyzed by the brokenness of our world but to *do the work* confident that God, who loves us, is co-laboring with us and will triumph over brokenness in the end.

Perhaps you will be moved by these reflections. If so, you have something to talk to God about and something that you can do with others that will move us toward a more sustainable world environment.

Love Your Enemies

Along the same lines comes a quite recent book by Arthur C. Brooks (no relation to David), the former president of the American Enterprise Institute, *Love Your Enemies: How Decent People Can Save America from the Culture of Contempt* (New York: HarperCollins, 2019). In an inviting style and with great verve and energy he shows how the culture of contempt threatens to destroy democracy in America and with great examples and down-to-earth recommendations helps readers to do what Jesus asks of all of us: to love our enemies as well as our friends.

Brooks is an unabashed conservative on social issues, but he advocates openness to those with opposite stances toward public policy rather than the now-prevalent culture of contempt for those who oppose one's views. He is also a disturber of the comfortable among us who are content to be with like-minded people only. A wake-up call indeed.

Krista Tippett

Krista Tippett has also become a prophet for me. I have not listened to her weekly radio show, *On Being*, but I have read her three books based on interviews on the show. She, too, constantly reminds her hearers and readers of what our world needs at the present, critical time, and the message is similar to that of both David Brooks and Arthur Brooks. I found her books to be loving, demanding goads to my conscience and my heart. Here is just one example.

In *Becoming Wise: An Inquiry into the Mystery and Art of Living*, she cites the well-known Benedictine sister Joan Chittister, who tells the story of how fragile St. Benedict's early attempts were at setting up small communities of monks who would remain in their monasteries but welcome all those who came to them. No one could have predicted that a thousand years later in the Middle Ages his monasteries would save Western civilization's culture. Tippett remarks that she is heartened by this story and needs to be reminded that there are many such beginnings now that might change the world as we know it. She then goes on to write:

> Still, I am dazzled by the great good I can discern everywhere out there. . . . I have a heart full, arms full, a mind brimful and bursting with a sense of what is healing

us even as I write, even when we don't know it and haven't asked for it. And I do mean healing: not curing, not solving, not fixing, but creating the opportunity for deepened life together, for growing more wise and more whole, not just older, not just smarter. . . .

I'm constantly shedding the assumption that a skeptical point of view is the most intellectually credible. Intellect does not function in opposition to mystery; tolerance is not more pragmatic than love; and cynicism is not more reasonable than hope. Unlike almost every worthwhile thing in life, cynicism is easy. It's never proven wrong by the corruption or the catastrophe. It's not generative. It judges things as they are, but does not lift a finger to try to shift them.[16]

In this book Tippett regularly cites examples of points of light that belie the doomsayers, but she also knows that hope is a fragile virtue that does not deny the darkness around us. Hope is precisely that, hope in a future that is endangered all the time. I find in her another instance of how God continually is a difficult friend who, even in criticizing us, loves us passionately.

What do you think? Have you found any writers or media people who push you at least a little to move out of your comfort zone and into a stance that might move acrimony to dialogue? Have you thought that such people were instruments of God for you? Perhaps these reflections will encourage you to engage in a good conversation with God about your own reactions to our world.

America's Original Sin

This academic year (2019–2020) the national office of the Ignatian Volunteer Corps has asked all those taking part in that program to read Jim Wallis's *America's Original Sin: Racism, White Privilege, and the Bridge to a New America.* After I had finished this book, I received his volume and read it eagerly. It discomforts the comfortable as God does. Moreover, it touches on one of the deepest problems we face in the United States. So, I decided to include a reference to it in this chapter. Jim Wallis is an Evangelical Protestant minister and founder of Sojourners, a publishing platform, organization, and global network whose mission is to put faith into action for social justice. This book discomfited me. It is a clarion call for American Christians to get in touch with the reality that people who are identified in this country as "white" are privileged in many, many ways at the expense of those identified as "black" or "brown." Wallis notes that America is one of the most racially diverse nations in the world, a fact that "is essential to our greatness." He then goes on to write:

> Ironically, and tragically, American diversity began with acts of violent racial oppression that I am calling

"America's original sin"—the theft of land from Indigenous people who were either killed or removed and the enslavement of millions of Africans who became America's greatest economic resource—in building a new nation. The theft of land and the violent exploitation of labor were embedded in America's origins.[17]

Wallis takes readers through all the ways that racism still continues to hurt us all, and he urges Christians to pray to God for help and to work to overcome the effects of our "original sin." Jim Wallis is a loving discomforter of all of us who are too comfortable with the effects of this original sin. Just as we are mostly unconscious of the effects of original sin and need the help of God and God's helpers to become aware of them, so too, we need the help of God and of believers like Wallis to become aware of the effects of the original sin of racism in the United States. Wallis does discomfort the comfortable, but clearly with love, as God discomforts us.

Saint Óscar Romero

You might say that, during his early life as a priest, Óscar Romero was a comforter of the comfortable, even after he became archbishop of San Salvador. But the killing of his good friend, Fr. Rutilio Grande, SJ, in 1977 opened his heart and mind to the suffering of the vast majority of the people of El Salvador. There was no doubt that Rutilio was killed because he was helping the poor he served to believe that they were beloved children of God who deserved to live a better life than the bare subsistence relegated to them. Romero went to the village where Grande was to be buried and from that day onward became a comforter of the afflicted poor and a discomfort to those who kept them under their thumb.

He regularly preached on Sundays on Christ's love for the poor and the Christian's duty to act justly. As a result of these sermons, which were broadcast to the whole country, he became a thorn in the side of the governing party and the wealthy landowners and was repeatedly threatened. Three years after the murder of Rutilio Grande, Romero himself was assassinated while celebrating Mass.

Being an image of God who discomfits the too comfortable has its consequences. Óscar Romero followed the same path as his Lord Jesus and suffered a similar fate from the powers that wanted to conserve their power at any cost.

Does this reflection remind you of other afflicters of the comfortable? Do you feel any desire to speak with God about this reflection?

The Need for Discernment

One thing I must say here is that we need to be discerning about the discomfort we sometimes feel as we face the enormous challenges of this time in history. I have noted in myself a feeling of despair and a desire to forget the whole thing when I am bombarded by all the misery in the world and the needs of so many. I have come to believe that this reaction is not of God, because it leads nowhere but to despondency and retreat from doing anything. I'm not God, I have to tell myself. I cannot save the world, or any part of it. I have to ask myself, "What can I do in these concrete circumstances and at my age?"

This question, or something like it, brings me back to the real world and to wonder what I can do in my little part of it to make things better. I suppose that's why I was so taken by Tippett's comments in response to Joan Chittister's story of Benedict. We are only small points of light in this dark world, where the real light is provided by God in Jesus Christ, who is the Light of the world.

Maybe you are moved to speak with God about your own discomfort.

12

God and Anger

I opened the last chapter with stories of God's anger at the Israelites. Two of the readings for the liturgy on the Fourteenth Sunday after Pentecost in Cycle B (the day before I began this chapter) got me thinking of how God reacts to our rather regular infidelities. I began my homily by telling this story.

A Father's Anger at His Son

Some years ago, at a retreat house in Texas, I met a Mexican American man who told me of an incident with his son when the son was a teenager and beginning to feel his oats. One evening the boy began to argue about something his father wanted him to do and eventually raised his fist as if to challenge his father to a fight. The father was filled with great love for his boy but also a hot anger. Instead of engaging in a verbal or physical fight, however, he said something like this: "Son, as long as you stay in this house, you have to obey me and your mother. If you don't want to do that, then you must leave now."

The father said that his heart was breaking as he spoke, but he felt that he had to do it for the sake of the boy and of their family. The boy started toward the door, then stopped; his face fell, and he said, "But where will I go?" His father answered, "Son, go to bed now, and we'll talk about this in the morning." The boy went to bed.

The father told me that even at the time, but especially now during this retreat, he thought of how God must feel when he sees us in rebellion and hurting ourselves and others. Great love and, at the same time, great anger and sorrow, and all these feelings are directed at the rebel. I got the father's permission to use this story in other retreats and in writing.

Does the story remind you of anything in your own family history when something similar happened? Perhaps as a teenager, you were like the rebellious son, and your father or mother had to chastise you. Sometimes, of course, parents go overboard, taking teenage rebellion too personally and seeming to lose any love for their teenagers. But perhaps we can cut them some slack and understand their anger as motivated not only by personal affront but also by their deep love for their children and their desire to keep them on the right path. Perhaps, too, you were reminded of your own reactions to your own teenagers.

Do you want to talk with God about any of your own reactions and even the times when you lost your cool under the pressure of raising teenagers? Whatever you remember, you can talk over with God and take some time to hear a response of some kind.

The Scripture Readings

Now to the readings that prompted the telling of the story. The first was from the call of the prophet Ezekiel. I am using the NRSV translation, not the one used in the Roman Catholic liturgy.

He said to me: O mortal, stand up on your feet, and I will speak with you. And when he spoke to me, a spirit entered into me and set me on my feet; and I heard him speaking to me. He said to me, Mortal, I am sending you to the people of Israel, to a nation of rebels who have rebelled against me; they and their ancestors have transgressed against me to this very day. The descendants are impudent and stubborn. I am sending you to them, and you shall say to them, "Thus says the Lord GOD." Whether they hear or refuse to hear (for they are a rebellious house), they shall know that there has been a prophet among them. (Ezekiel 2:1–5)

As you read or hear these words to the prophet, what tone of voice do you hear God use as he calls the Israelites rebels, impudent, and stubborn? I hear strong anger but also an undertone of great love. God still wants to send another prophet to give the Israelites another chance.

Do you want to say anything to God? Were you reminded of any incident in your own life by the story of the Mexican American father or by this reading from Ezekiel? Again, do you want to say anything to God? Or to ask God anything?

The Hebrew Bible is filled with stories of the Israelites' failure to trust God and of their search for another god to take the place of the God of Abraham, of Isaac, and of Jacob when they were faced with difficulties. In the desert, after God had saved them from slavery to the Egyptians, they are depicted as constantly complaining and wishing that they had remained slaves in Egypt. At one point, it's almost funny when they pine for the leeks and onions and garlic of Egypt instead of "this manna." God often seems to regret having chosen them to be his people, threatening to leave them to destruction at one point, before Moses intervenes to change God's mind. Can you now understand these outbursts of anger on God's part as motivated by deep love and concern for these people and for you?

The Gospel reading for that same Sunday was from Mark 6:1–6:

> [Jesus] left that place and came to his home town, and his disciples followed him. On the sabbath he began to teach in the synagogue, and many who heard him were astounded. They said, "Where did this man get all this? What is this wisdom that has been given to him? What deeds of power are being done by his hands! Is not this the carpenter, the son of Mary and brother of James and Joses and Judas and Simon, and are not his sisters here with us?" And they took offense at him. Then Jesus said to them, "Prophets are not without honor, except in their home town, and among their own kin, and in their own house." And he could do no deed of power there, except that he laid his hands on a few sick people and cured them. And he was amazed at their unbelief.

Jesus has come back to Nazareth, the town where he grew up, and runs into a wall of resistance there when he begins to teach in the local synagogue. You know how it can be when a local boy makes good. People who remember him as a boy and teenager start to mutter, wondering where he "got the nerve to think he's better than us and can tell us how to live or what God has in mind." It says that Jesus "was amazed at their unbelief."

As you imagined this scene, what was Jesus like? How did he react to their resentment? What fueled his "amazement": Sadness? Hurt? Anger? Maybe you want to ask him about his reactions. If so, go ahead.

Let's suppose that his amazement was the result of a mix of all these emotions: sadness because he did love them, hurt because these were personal attacks, anger because they were stupidly missing out on what the Israelites had been hoping for and dreaming about for centuries—the coming of the Messiah, the Anointed One. Jesus is, we believe, not only that Messiah but also the very Son of God, God's final gift of self to this world. Rejecting him meant rejecting the one best hope they had of enjoying what both God and they (and we) want: a world where all of us live in harmony with God, with one another, and with the whole created universe.

I can easily imagine Jesus at this moment torn by sadness, hurt, and anger as he sees his beloved neighbors, friends, and, perhaps, some of his own extended family turning against God's greatest gift of love. What do you think?

Father of Orphans and Protector of Widows

In the Bible, God is depicted as "Father of orphans and protector of widows" (Psalm 68:5) and as quite angry when they and others are treated unkindly. For example, in Isaiah we read:

> Ah, you who make iniquitous decrees,
>> who write oppressive statutes,
> to turn aside the needy from justice
>> and to rob the poor of my people of their right,
> that widows may be your spoil,
>> and that you may make the orphans your prey!
> What will you do on the day of punishment,
>> in the calamity that will come from far away?
> To whom will you flee for help,
>> and where will you leave your wealth,
> so as not to crouch among the prisoners
>> or fall among the slain?
> For all this his anger has not turned away;
>> his hand is stretched out still.
>
> —Isaiah 10:1–4

In other passages, God's anger against his people is stirred by their treatment of aliens in their midst. God reminds them that they were once aliens in Egypt themselves. How do you react to this passage? Does the mistreatment of widows, orphans, and the poor incite your anger?

Refugees in Our Midst

Recently (summer of 2018), many in the United States were outraged to see and hear how the children of refugees seeking asylum in this country had been torn from their parents and kept in cages far apart from them. Perhaps this angry outrage was a pale reflection of God's reaction to what was happening. Throughout the Bible, God is described as a God of justice, especially of justice for the less fortunate of this world. Thus it is not farfetched, I believe, to see in the anger of so many Americans about the treatment of refugees in the summer of 2018 a reflection of God's anger. What do you think?

You probably noticed that in the Isaiah passage God's anger is motivated by his love for the downtrodden, people such as widows and orphans. Very often, such love is what seems to motivate God's anger. Even God's anger at the Israelites when they worshipped false gods was motivated by love; God knew that the worship of false gods would lead only to disaster for them.

So, when we find ourselves outraged at injustice against others, we need to check to find out the source of our anger. Is it motivated by love for those who suffer the injustice, or is it more a wish to harm the perpetrators of the injustice? If we find that the latter predominates, it might be wise to ask God's help to keep our motivations more in tune with his.

Mind you, some anger at the perpetrators is legitimate and even a reflection of God's angry reactions to injustice, but we have to remember that God loves *everyone*, even the perpetrators of injustice, and God wants their conversion. I've noticed that sometimes my anger clearly wants those who perpetrate great injustices to suffer at least as much as their victims have suffered; it does not enter my mind to hope for their conversion when I am so angry. I have needed to remember what Jesus said in the Sermon on the Mount:

> You have heard that it was said, "You shall love your neighbor and hate your enemy." But I say to you, Love your enemies and pray for those who persecute you, so that you may be children of your Father in heaven; for he makes his sun rise on the evil and on the good, and sends rain on the righteous and on the unrighteous. . . . Be perfect, therefore, as your heavenly Father is perfect. (Matthew 5:43–48)

God's anger is always tempered by love for all concerned. Let's pray that our own anger at injustice will always be tempered by love and thus truly image God.

When do we encounter such true images of God as expressed through anger? Well, that Texas teenager met God in his father, didn't he? Bill Russell and I met God when Darrell Jones, the ex-prisoner mentioned in chapters 2 and 6, asked us, with tears in his eyes, to pray that he would be able to forgive those who had unjustly put him in prison for thirty-two years.

Anger in the Civil Rights Movement in the United States

In *Becoming Wise: An Inquiry into the Mystery and Art of Living*, Krista Tippett reminds us of what a miracle of grace the nonviolent movement for civil rights begun by Martin Luther King Jr. in the 1960s and 1970s was. Tippett's book features outtakes from many of her radio interviews. In one she interviewed John Lewis, now an elderly Congressman from Georgia, about the time when, as a young man, he worked with Martin Luther King Jr. Reading about it was for me a sign of God's presence.

Those of us who were alive in the 1960s and 1970s remember the marches led by King and others to protest the treatment of African American people. We watched the marches on TV and read about them in the newspapers, but most of us had no idea of the kind of training and discipline that went into the way the marchers acted when attacked.

Tippett's book offered some idea from what John Lewis and others told her.

> The movement they brought into being was a spiritual confrontation in the most expansive sense of that word, first and foremost within oneself and then with the world outside. For weeks, months, before any sit-in or march or ride, they studied the Bible and Gandhi, Aristotle and Thoreau. They internalized practical, physical disciplines of courtesy and conduct—kindness, eye contact, coat and tie, dresses; no unnecessary words. . . . They engaged in intense role-playing—"social drama"—whites putting themselves in the role of blacks being harassed, black activists putting themselves in the shoes of policemen feeling threatened and under orders to gain control.
>
> This was love as a way of being, not a feeling, which transcended grievance and painstakingly transformed violence.[18]

These activists worked at developing virtue. They knew that what they were getting into would be difficult and would test them. And so they learned to practice virtue even under very, very difficult circumstances—for example, being bitten by a vicious dog sent at them by a policeman. There is a lesson here for all of us. Virtue does require work and a great deal of patience and practice. Moreover, I notice that the discipline of love tempered the anger that also motivated the people of this movement.

In a response to one of Tippett's questions, John Lewis himself gives us an insight into how he was touched by God through others. When he was eleven, he traveled from rural Alabama to Buffalo with some family members, his first time out of the South. "And being there gave me hope. I wanted to believe, and I did believe, that things would get better. Later I discovered that you have to have this sense of faith that what you're moving toward is already done. It's already happened." Tippett asked, "And live as if?" He answered:

> And you live as if you're already there, that you're already in that community, part of that sense of one family, one house. If you visualize it, if you can even have faith that it's there, for you it is already there. And during the early days of the movement, I believed that the only true and real integration for that sense of the beloved community existed within the movement itself. Because in the final analysis, we did become a circle of trust, a band of brothers and sisters. It didn't matter whether you were black or white. It didn't matter whether you came from the North to the South, or whether you're a Northerner or Southerner. We were one.[19]

Lewis here was speaking of what God desires for our world. Moreover, what Lewis says of belief is, as far as I am concerned, what Christians mean by believing in the life, death, and resurrection of Jesus. That life, death, and resurrection changed the world. It means that the new heavens and the new earth are already here. Christians are asked to believe this, not just in words, but by how they live. We are asked to live now as though the beloved community is already here.

This belief is what made the early Christians so attractive, and, of course, also dangerous to the establishment. This is, I believe, what Lewis experienced in the early days of the movement.

The Novel *Plainsong*

Kent Haruf's novel *Plainsong* gave me another experience of God and anger. Here's what happened. In my rereading of the book just before bedtime, I came to the part where three teenagers, two boys and the girlfriend of one of them, forcibly push their teacher Guthrie's two young boys into their car after a movie. They intend to scare them because one of the teenagers, a high school basketball star, was very angry at Guthrie. As a result of an altercation with Guthrie he was suspended from school, thus being unable to play in the big game with their main high school rival. He had also done none of the work for Guthrie's American history class, and Guthrie flunked him. Hence, he could not graduate with his class. The three take the two boys out into the country five miles from the little town of Holt and drop them off to walk home. To make matters worse, they take off the boys' shoes and all their clothes and throw them into the nearby field.

The next day, a Sunday, Guthrie confronts the teenager at his home. The mother of the young man comes out and berates Guthrie. When the husband comes out, Guthrie tells them what their boy has done to his boys.

I was getting so upset by all this that I realized I would find it hard to sleep if I kept going. So I turned out the lights and started my usual prayer before falling sleep. "Father, Son, and Holy Spirit" on the intake of breath. When I started to move toward the outbreath, I thought of what I had just been reading. Many times my outbreath prayer is, "Help me to love my neighbor." I thought of this teenager and his parents and realized that I could not pray to love them.

So I told God this and asked him, "Do you love them?" I didn't hear words, but this is what God seemed to say, "Yes, I do, but I don't approve of all they do." I thought about this and realized that I had often said and wrote that God loves everyone, even Hitler, Pol Pot, Idi Amin, and other people who have caused untold misery in this world. So at least I could ask to love this family. Here is another instance where God's presence comes from an unlikely source: reading a novel.

Can you recall ever reading a newspaper or a novel or watching a movie and feeling so angry at someone in the story that you wanted them to suffer? You also know from experience my reactions to the scene from *Plainsong*. Often the writers have such reactions in mind as they write, because they, too, feel that way about what has happened.

Have you ever wondered about such reactions? I have often thought that my reactions of anger might be a pale resemblance of God's reactions to grave injustices. The question, however, that my own experience raises for me, and perhaps for you, is this: Is the desire to see the other suffer in tune with God's anger? What came to me that evening was an answer to this question. At least in my case, the desire for revenge was not in tune with God's full reaction.

What are your experiences with anger, even at a fictitious character or situation? What do you think these experiences have to tell you? Can you bring this matter to prayer?

I believe that anger against injustice and cruelty is a gift of God. But we need to grow into mature human beings made in the image and likeness of God. The best way to grow into this maturity is by engaging with God about our aggressive tendencies. That is, we need to let God know about all our angry and aggressive reactions, even the ones we don't like, and to ask God's help to become more like his Son, Jesus, who himself grew into a mature human being with an aggressive drive. God has asked us to become like Jesus and to join in the great adventure that is creation and to be God's images as mature human beings whose aggressive drives are in tune with what God hopes for.

The Conclusion of the Father's Story

To end this chapter where we began, let me tell you that at the end of his story the Mexican American man told me that he and his son, now an adult with his own growing family, are close friends. Again, I see in that ending God's presence.

Isn't that the relationship God wants with every one of us "obstinate and impudent" rebels? Perhaps you want to talk with God the Father or with Jesus about your reactions to this chapter and to this ending. Never hesitate to tell God everything that is in your heart.

13

God and Humor

My first impulse was to title this chapter "God Must Have a Funny Bone," but it seemed too flippant. I have often referred to the humor in the exchanges between Abram/Abraham and Sarai/Sarah and God. When Abraham falls down in laughter at the preposterous idea that he, at 100, and Sarah, at 90, would have a son the following year and asks God to bless the only son he will ever have, Ishmael, God also seems to get into the humor by saying that they will call their new son Isaac, which means "Laughter," and then says, in effect, "As for Ishmael, I'll take care of him. Don't worry about him." I have been told by people who know Hebrew that the original Hebrew of the Bible contains many instances of humor such as this.

Jesus seems to have had a sense of humor as shown by his use of nicknames: Peter (or Rocky, as the late Daniel

Harrington noted) for Simon, and "Sons of Thunder" for James and John. I interpret the latter as an acknowledgment by Jesus of how Zebedee, their father, reacted when Jesus took both of them away from the family fishing business. It seems that Jesus had a fine sense of humor.

Humor seems to be a common trait of all of us human beings. I like to think that our sense of humor is another way in which we are images of God. Actually, perhaps only a sense of humor could explain God's continued love for and patience with us—his messy, contradictory, and recalcitrant children.

I do remember that my parents' sense of humor seems to have saved their love for us children. For instance, I can still remember my mother chasing me around the table to punish me and then when I stopped and she did punish me, saying "Why did you stop, you *ohnchick*?" [my spelling of her Irish word, which, I believe, means "imp"].

Let's take it for granted that God somehow has a sense of humor and that our own sense of humor is his gift to us as part of our inheritance as images of God. In this chapter I would like to point out instances where humor clearly showed the presence of God and thus open your mind and heart to noticing how present God is in humorous situations.

The Infant Is Missing

In the first chapter I mentioned Carl Scovel's collection of the best radio sermons from his twenty years of weekly Sunday radio broadcasts. When he gave me a copy of this book, *Never Far from Home*, he noted that everyone's favorite was titled "The Stolen Infant." King's Chapel, where he was pastor for over thirty years, is Unitarian. Carl introduces this story by noting, with wry humor, that at his home on 63 Beacon Street, his daughters were not happy with the fact that he kept the temperature quite low during the winter. Then he talks about what happened at the Christmas Eve services. With some trepidation that year he placed a terra cotta crèche with Mary, Joseph, the Christ child, shepherds and kings on the communion table for the Christmas Eve and Day services. The Christmas Eve services all went smoothly, and he was relieved at the response of the congregation. But after the 10:30 p.m. service, the verger came to him to say that the Christ child was missing from the crèche. After some searching, Carl found a note in the crèche that read, "We've got Jesus. Turn up the heat at 63 Beacon Street, and you can have Him back for the morning service." As I read, I broke out laughing. Carl concludes:

> The heat went up at the parsonage, the infant reappeared, and everything returned to normal. Well, not

quite. The benevolent despot of 63 Beacon Street sits less certainly upon his throne. That is probably not surprising.

No monarch, indeed no despot, can ever be quite sure of his rule when the child has been born.[20]

It's a wonderful story, well told. And note the last line, which so cleverly and deftly refers to what happens when God becomes a child.

Can you remember any time when humor so easily made God's presence known to you? Maybe you would like to talk with God about that time or about your reaction to this story.

Humor as an Indicator That You Are Comfortable with People

I've noticed that my sense of humor is most evident when I am comfortable, even friendly, with those around me. In these circumstances I like to josh with my friends, and they with me. As I think about it, the humor in the stories of Abraham and Sarah in the book of Genesis seems to come when both of them are more comfortable with God. At the beginning they just obey without a murmur; only later do they engage in humorous banter with God, and God with them.

The closer I am to people, the easier I find it to be humorous with them. Do you notice this? It may well be that humor and real love for others go hand in hand. Just as tears seem to me often a sign of God's presence, humor may also be such a sign.

As a matter of fact, I find that I cannot josh humorously with those with whom I am uncomfortable or do not like. The reason is that I am not sure that such people will grasp that I mean the humor as a way of showing how much I care for them. Mind you, I am not shy about telling people I like or love them, but I think that I often use humor to say the same thing. I suspect that God likes this aspect of my way of being with people and, perhaps, wishes that I were able to be as comfortable with all those I meet. Does this make sense to you?

Humor Helps Us Deal with Difficulties

During my recent stint in our health center, I noticed that humor was one of the ways I coped with the pain and the inability to do things for myself as usual. I would casually call myself "gimp" and laugh at my inability to walk steadily, for example, as a way to lighten my own mood and to make others more comfortable. I found that the humor of others, especially that of my friend and Good Samaritan, Bill Russell, SJ, helped me keep up my spirits.

Remember the homily by Fr. Rich Bollman, SJ, for the funeral liturgy of his good friend and mine, Fr. James Keegan, SJ? Jim, who was crippled by the ravages of Parkinson's disease for the last years of his life, was an example to me, and to others, I'm sure, by the way that he dealt with the ever-continuing restrictions the illness put on him. Often, he, too, dealt with the pain and growing restrictions with humor.

Jim was a poet, and he wrote several poems about his reactions to the disease. In these poems he expressed his sadness and anger at the losses the disease was causing, but he also wrote with humor in a few of these poems.

In the one I choose to share here, he starts by recalling how as a novice working in the laundry, he and other novices laughed at the food stains left on the garments of the older Jesuits and then goes on to talk about one of the effects of his disease on his own clothes. I hope it brings a smile or a laugh to you as it does to me.

> Asia
> The old fathers' shirts would tumble out of the
>   dryers
>   just before ours went in.

They once were white but after a thousand washings
they emerged yellow and brown like old *New York
    Times.*

We laughed.
Down the front ran juice- or butter-shaped
   continents and rivers, natural borders,
great beasts circling jungles or Leviathan
   frolicking to no one's harm,
etched forever into the tumble dried cloth.
Praise for last week's ranch dressing,
   chicken stew, squash pie.

We laughed.
Between the teeth of a fading alligator hung
   a pasta sauce lamb,
no longer red but, with its many deaths
   a musty rose.
The beast and its prey were one.
We found the only still-white spot on
   an otherwise indelible
yellow t-shirt and declared it The North Pole.

We laughed. There was only Asia to discover now.
Last night at the end of dinner,
a fresh cut of salmon with peas, carrots, and rice
   had tilted my balance.
I looked with disgust at the trail of pink fish
pursued by a posse of green peas

from my shirt down to the edge of the plate,
the lip of the table and down,
into areas which my crowded bib could not guard.
A friend's voice, from the left:
   "You did fine work wrestling the salmon."
I laughed. We laughed.[21]

Have you been helped to bear difficult situations by humor?
Then perhaps you, too, have realized with some surprise that
God loves a good laugh. Do you want to laugh with God about
some of your memories or about what happened to Jim Keegan?

Humor and the Relaxation of Tension

Have you ever noticed how humor not only indicates how
relaxed you are with the people around you but also brings
about a relaxation of tension? I have been in any number
of relatively tense situations when someone said something
that brought on laughter in all of us. Almost immediately
the tension seemed to disappear. I believe that I learned this
early in my life and have used humor to ease tensions all
my life.

(Mind you, it does not always work. Once when I was
a boy, my mother was very angry with my father. When
she came into our flat, I made a humorous remark, hoping
to reduce the tension. She was not pleased and gave me a

smack. I learned the need to pick the times of interventions very carefully.)

If I'm right about humor as an easer of tensions, perhaps here again we have a surprising sign of God's presence to us. God, perhaps with a sense of humor, gave us this gift as a way of easing tensions that might lead to long hostilities and even permanent estrangements. Maybe you will now sense God's presence when you experience humor. I certainly have.

By the way, it seems that animals also use humor to defuse tension. In *Mama's Last Hug*, Frans de Waal gives an example of three adult male chimpanzees who were showing all the signs of being ready for a battle with one another, when one of them played a joke on the other, clearly laughing. The others caught on and after this, the three of them galloped around, punching one another playfully and laughing hoarsely. De Waal notes that laughter signals not only to one's buddies but also to the outside world that you want to ease things.

Humor among animals, as in humans, indicates ease and good relations. We can say that humor is a gift of God to help us get along with one another—in effect, to love one another.

The next time you laugh, pay attention to it. You may well find that you are experiencing the presence of our surprising God. Perhaps you now want to have a conversation with God about how humor has eased some of the tensions in your own life.

Thank You for Turning Off Your Phone

I found the following on the Internet. It was accompanied by the line, "This notice can now be found in all French churches" which I doubt very much. But it would be fine by me if it were true. I include both the French and the English translation for your benefit.

> En entrant dans cette église, il est possible que vous entendiez l'appel de Dieu.
> Par contre, il n'est pas susceptible de vous contacter par téléphone.
> Merci d'avoir éteint votre téléphone.
> Si vous souhaitez parler à Dieu, entrez, choisissez un endroit tranquille et parle lui.
> Si vous souhaitez le voir, envoyez-lui un SMS en conduisant.

> Translation:
> It is possible that on entering this church, you may hear the call of God.

> On the other hand, it is not likely that he will
>   contact you by phone.
> Thank you for turning off your phone.
> If you would like to talk to God, come in, choose a
>   quiet place, and talk to him.
> If you would like to see him, send him a text while
>   driving.

If you found this notice in a church, wouldn't you laugh at it and find this church a very attractive place? Don't you think that God would be pleased too? Perhaps you have something you want to say to God.

Humor Is the Spice of Life

Carol Johannes, OP, a good friend and a spiritual director, wrote me the following:

> Then there are all the really funny ideas people have about God. Sometimes I think of God or Jesus laughing out loud, as when one of my directees told me she had never prayed to God, only to the angels, because God is so busy.
>
> Finally, it seems to me that whenever we have an experience that delights us because it's really hilarious and makes us laugh until we almost cry, somehow or other that experience is of God. These moments lift our

spirits, make our hearts light, and transform life from grimness to joy. I think that's often God's work.

I'm sure that you've noticed how humor wants to be shared; humor is not solipsistic. When you hear a funny joke, don't you want to tell a friend or anyone who will listen? I suspect that God put the funny bone in us so that we would enjoy one another's company. I'll bet it's your experience that humor reigns where people enjoy one another's company. Humor is, very often, a form of love, and God is love, as the first letter of John has it. Maybe you are moved to have a talk with God about your own humorous experiences.

14

How Do We Know We Are
Experiencing God?

Near the end of chapter 11 of Matthew's Gospel, Jesus prays aloud to his Father in words that reveal a great deal about his inner life. Indeed, more and more is revealed with each reading, it seems to me. Here is what he prayed:

> At that time Jesus said, "I thank you, Father, Lord of heaven and earth, because you have hidden these things from the wise and the intelligent and have revealed them to infants; yes, Father, for such was your gracious will. All things have been handed over to me by my Father; and no one knows the Son except the Father, and no one knows the Father except the Son and anyone to whom the Son chooses to reveal him."
>
> "Come to me, all you that are weary and are carrying heavy burdens, and I will give you rest. Take my yoke upon you, and learn from me; for I am gentle and

humble in heart, and you will find rest for your souls. For my yoke is easy, and my burden is light." (Matthew 11:25–30)

My most recent hearing of this passage occurred fairly soon after I had started work on this book. So, my reflections were probably affected by its theme. At any rate, I began to reflect on Jesus' experience of himself as Messiah and Son of God. Remember that Jesus is a human being like us in all things except sin, as Paul says. He, like us, is created as an image of God. I ask you to reflect with me now with that always in mind. I tried to imagine what it was like for Jesus, the human being, to have the kinds of experiences that would convince him that he was the Messiah promised for centuries to Israel, and, even more astounding, that he and the unfathomable God of Israel and the world were in some mysterious way one. It must have raised questions in his mind. After all, according to Mark, his family at one point thought he had gone crazy and came to bring him back home to Nazareth (Mark 3:21, 31–34), and the scribes from Jerusalem believed him possessed by Beelzebul (Mark 3:22–27). Isn't it possible that Jesus himself, as a human being, wondered whether his family and the scribes were right? He was, as well, having experiences of God that ran counter to what the leaders of his religion were teaching about God. Remember that Jesus was a human being like us.

Jesus Had to Discern God's Movement in His Life

How did Jesus decide that he had to trust his experiences as coming from his Father? How does any human being decide that the experiences of God they have are genuine? Of course, we can consult someone in authority in our church or someone who is learned and insightful about the history of spirituality. But ultimately each of us is responsible for his or her own soul. We cannot pin our souls to anyone else's back. We must decide whether our experiences are genuine. In the history of spirituality, making such decisions is called the "discernment of spirits" to decide what in our experience is from God and what is not.

However, Jesus was dealing with something unprecedented in the history of the world. Granted, he had the example of predecessors such as Abraham, Moses, and many prophets who had to decide that the unprecedented messages they were experiencing came from God and to act upon that revelation. But no sane person in the history of the world had ever had to discern whether he or she was God in human flesh. So, I tend to believe that Jesus had to struggle interiorly with conflicting thoughts and feelings about his experiences in order to come to the decision that he was indeed the Messiah and Son of God.

One can see the temptations in the desert as at least a part of this struggle. In the Gospels of Matthew, Mark, and Luke the temptations scene comes directly after Jesus' baptism by John in the Jordan, which many commentators see as either the time when Jesus came to the conclusion that he was the Messiah or as a confirmation of a decision made earlier after some time of discernment.

Right after the baptism, Jesus goes into the desert for forty days, where he is tempted by Satan. These temptations can be understood as temptations about how to be the Messiah: to use his powers to feed himself; to throw himself from the temple, trusting that God would save him and he would be famous; and, finally, to use the tactics of the enemy to win power over the nations to bring on the reign of God. Jesus saw through each of these temptations and decided that they were not from his Father.

I believe that Jesus, too, had to pay attention to his experiences of life and then figure out what in these experiences was from the Father, what was from other influences—his mood that day, how his digestive system was working, his memories, what he was concerned about at the time, or

Satan, the enemy of his soul. In other words, as a human being he had to distinguish what came from his Father as opposed to what came from other sources in the various experiences of his day. At least this is the best I can do to understand his human experience.

Those who think that Jesus knew everything, including the future, are only speculating about such things. No human being has any idea how God knows the future or anything else because God is precisely God, the mysterious Other whom no finite being can ever understand. What we have some knowledge of is what it means to be human, and human beings do not know the future and are limited in their understanding even of the world we inhabit.

So, to get some idea of how Jesus came to the kind of knowledge of himself that he had, we can only speculate from our own human experience. That's why I believe that Jesus had to do what we have to do in order to decide that he was the long-awaited Messiah promised to the Jewish people and the Son of God: He had to pay attention to his experiences and then decide what was from the Father in them, what not.

Why am I pressing this point now? I believe that God communicates to each of us human beings through our human experience. Throughout the book I have been pointing to various experiences we all have in order to point out where other human beings and other creatures have been images of God for us, have been God's communication to us. In addition, we have looked at how each of us has been an image of God for others. To get the point across I have been urging you to pay attention to your experience, to notice differences between some experiences and others, and to decide what came from God in the experiences and what did not come from God. Throughout I have been urging you to see yourselves and others as sacraments of God's presence and communication to our world now.

On the day I heard the words of Matthew's Gospel that began this chapter, I thought that you might be encouraged to know that Jesus himself had to discern his various experiences just as we have to. In addition, I hope that this chapter will help us all realize how much God has riding on us and our discernment. Think of how much God had riding on Jesus, on Mary of Nazareth and Joseph, on Abraham and Sarah, on Moses, and on the prophets.

Well, we are in that same line! God has entrusted us human beings with being his feeling, thinking, and willing images in this world. God wants human beings to join him freely and willingly, as only we can do, in the great work of bringing to completion the creation that began billions of years ago: "In the beginning when God created the heavens and the earth . . ." (Genesis 1:1). God thinks so highly of us humans as to become one of us, and God hopes that we will accept this underserved gift by living consciously and freely as friends of and images of God.

Some Indications That God Is in Your Experiences

One of the most influential ways of discerning God's ways comes from the *Spiritual Exercises* of Ignatius of Loyola. He asks people to look at their ordinary way of life and decide whether we are trying to live a life in harmony with God's desires. (I presume that you or anyone reading this book is trying to live a life in harmony with God.)

First let's look at what Ignatius says about those who are not on the right path. The "enemy of human nature," Ignatius's term for Satan, gives such people rationalizations to make them feel less concerned about their behavior; for example, to someone who is very wealthy and has just turned down a request to donate to his church's outreach to the homeless, "You're not such a bad guy; after all, remember that you gave a big donation to the church's drive to feed the poor" or, to someone who is troubled by his alcohol consumption, "You're not a falling-down drunk; you've never lost a day of work; you just need a drink or two to relax after work." (I know the latter strategy of the enemy because it kept me from facing my misuse of alcohol for many years.) The point is that the enemy is clever and will use any strategies that will quiet the nagging questions about our questionable behavioral habits.

How does the good spirit operate with people who are not on the same page as God? God's Spirit will try to get us to see the truth about our questionable behavioral patterns. We will experience a kind of nagging doubt about the course we are on; we won't be happy with ourselves after we have engaged in questionable behaviors. For example, often enough when I woke up the next day, I would question my drinking the night before. The Spirit of God won't let us stay comfortable with the status quo as long as these behaviors continue; God's Spirit wants us to be unblemished images of God, not just for the sake of others, but for our own sakes.

Now let's look at how these two spirits operate with those who are trying as best they can to be on the same page with God, people like you and other readers of this book. Here, as Ignatius writes, the two spirits act in just the opposite way to the way they act with people who are out of tune with God. The enemy of human nature will raise doubts and uncertainties, all of which tend to focus us on ourselves. "Who are you to think that God would speak with you?" "Typical of proud people like you to think you're special to God." "Sure, you're offering to help those poor people; but what's your motivation? Aren't you just in it to look good?"

A clear sign that such thoughts are not from God but from the enemy is that they are self-focused; they are all about me. Moreover, they lead nowhere but to feeling anxious and afraid. They do not lead to any positive action or, indeed, any action at all. The enemy of human nature seems to love seeing us spinning our inner wheels, getting nowhere.

With people on the right wavelength with God, the Spirit will arouse greater faith, hope, and love, and more élan for life. Such people will feel consoled and happy and not self-centered; their focus will be on God or on others rather than on themselves. Moreover, they will be moved toward positive action to make the world a better place.

In another helpful rule Ignatius counsels us not to make a major decision when down in the dumps. We cannot see things clearly in such a case and will probably make a rash decision. Wait until you are feeling better and have a clearer head and heart so that you can, with honesty, pay attention to all the factors involved in any major decision.

Remember, too, that the enemy can pose as your angelic friend. We can make rash decisions in a burst of fervor that we cannot carry out. For example, after hearing about the great need of the people in a foreign country, a man might volunteer to go there, even though he is terrible at learning other languages. In such a case, he might well become a liability to the people of that country.

You might also recall the criterion of beauty spoken of by Krista Tippett and her interviewees, the Muslim thinker Khaled Abou El Fadl and Rabbi Harold Schulweis. Tippett wrote: "Is it beautiful, or is it ugly? This question was proposed as a theological measuring stick, a credible litmus test. Does this action reveal a delight in this creation and in the image of a creative, merciful God who could have made it? Is it reverent with the mystery of that?"[22] This criterion, although not mentioned by Ignatius, might also help you to discern whether or not what you are experiencing is from God.

At all times, remember that all is grace, and that gratitude to God is, therefore, the primary religious attitude. Only God is God, thank God! God does indeed want us to cooperate in the great divine project that is our universe; but we are only small cogs, no matter what our talents. Gratitude that we can breathe, talk, help another in some way, or do anything is the only appropriate and sane response to being human. We exist only by the grace and gift of God. It is our honor and glory that we are invited to cooperate with God's project in our world, and that we can do it. So, thank God all the time.

And with that I say "Amen" and wish you the best as you continue this great adventure with God and continue to discover God's presence in the ordinary events of your life. God is good, all the time; all the time, God is good.

Acknowledgments

I am very grateful to all the people who have entrusted their stories to me and given me permission to use them in the book. Most have preferred to remain anonymous, and I have honored that preference. Others are mentioned by name, among them Tom Bradshaw; Paul Crowley, SJ; Mary Fitzgerald; Sr. Carol Johannes, OP; Jim Menno; Sr. Lisette Michaud; Sr. Ligita Ryliskyte, SJE; and Kevin White, SJ. To all I say thanks.

My sisters—Peggy, Mary, and Kathleen—have been a great support over my whole life; I have been blessed to have them as my sisters. Marika Geoghegan has been a friend and support for many years; she always encourages me to write and to take care of myself.

For the past fifteen years or more, Sr. Ellen Keane, SND, has been my spiritual director. A great gift to me.

Bill Russell, SJ, is a friend beyond compare and also makes me laugh; during my recovery from a recent fall, he dropped in to check on me at least four times every day. During that same recovery, Walter Smith, SJ, my superior, showed concern that went far beyond the call of duty. The staff of the Campion Health and Wellness Center was a sign of God's love for me that sometimes brought me to tears. I cannot thank them and all the staff at Campion Center enough. This book would not have been finished without their care for me. My brother Jesuits at Campion Center also were God's images for me as well by the care and concern that makes this large Jesuit community such a delightful place to live in, and to visit, as is corroborated by those who come to Campion Center for prayer and retreat.

Once I finished the book to my satisfaction, I asked seven friends to read it with care and to make suggestions. I am very grateful to Joseph A. Appleyard, SJ; Carol Johannes, OP; James J. Martin, SJ; Pam McCormick; William C. Russell, SJ; Simon E. Smith, SJ; and Judith Talvacchia for their generosity, care, and honesty.

Joe Durepos, in one of his last acts before his retirement as acquisitions editor at Loyola Press, gave me the green light to go ahead with the project. Vinita Wright, once again, has been an invaluable and very helpful editor at

Loyola Press. I thank both of them for their enthusiasm and their care for my manuscripts over the years. Indeed, the staff at Loyola Press has been very supportive; I thank them all.

Of course, my deepest gratitude is to God, without whom I would be nothing, quite literally.

Endnotes

1. Carl Scovel, *Never Far from Home: Stories from the Radio Pulpit* (Boston: Skinner House Books, 2016).

2. Scovel, *Never Far from Home*, 106.

3. Brian Doyle, *A Book of Uncommon Prayer: 100 Celebrations of the Miracle & Muddle of the Ordinary* (Notre Dame, IN: Sorin Books, 2014), 25–26.

4. Brian Doyle, *A Book of Uncommon Prayer*, 155–56.

5. Frederick Buechner, *The Eyes of the Heart: A Memoir of the Lost and Found* (San Francisco: HarperSanFrancisco, 1999), 97.

6. Kent Haruf, *Plainsong* (New York: Vintage Contemporaries, 1999), 78.

7. Krista Tippett, *Speaking of Faith: Why Religion Matters—and How to Talk About It* (New York: Penguin Books, 2007), 106.

8. Krista Tippett, *Speaking of Faith*, 96–99.

9. See www.americamagazine.org/politics-society/2016/12/07/my-family-disagrees-about-donald-trump-wont-divide-us.

10. Marcel Uwineza, *What the Rwandan Genocide Can Teach Us about Christian Hope*, www.americamagazine.org/issue/christian-hope.

11. David Brooks, "Fred Rogers and the Loveliness of the Little Good," *The New York Times*, July 5, 2018, A21, www.nytimes.com/2018/07/05/opinion/mister-fred-rogers-wont-you-be-my-neighbor.html.

12. Krista Tippett, *Speaking of Faith: Why Religion Matters—and How to Talk About It* (New York: Penguin Books, 2007), 196.

13. Krista Tippett, *Speaking of Faith*, 196–97.

14. Anne Lamott, *Help, Thanks, Wow: The Three Essential Prayers* (New York: Riverhead Books, 2012), 71.

15. David Brooks, "Cory Booker Finds His Moment," *The New York Times*, March 18, 2019, A27.

16. Krista Tippett, *Becoming Wise: An Inquiry into the Mystery and Art of Living* (New York: Penguin Books, 2017), 236.

17. James Wallis, *America's Original Sin: Racism, White Privilege, and the Bridge to a New America* (Grand Rapids, MI: Brazos Press, 2016), 9.

18. Krista Tippett, *Becoming Wise*, 110.

19. Krista Tippett, *Becoming Wise*, 111.

20. Carl Scovel, *Never Far from Home: Stories from the Radio Pulpit* (Boston: Skinner House Books, 2016), 44–46.

21. James M. Keegan, SJ, *These Hands: Poems by James M. Keegan, SJ*, edited with reflections by James M. Weiss and illustrated by Julie Gratz. (Weston, MA: Campion Center, 2017), 12–13.

22. Krista Tippett, *Speaking of Faith: Why Religion Matters—and How to Talk About It* (New York: Penguin Books, 2007), 197.

About the Author

William A. Barry, SJ, gives spiritual direction and retreats at Campion Center. He is the author of several popular books about Ignatian spirituality, including *A Friendship Like No Other*, *Praying the Truth*, and *An Invitation to Love*.